D0458075

EPISODE
ROBINSON

EPISODE #39
(PT 1 + PT 2)
NIL PORTER

DE #70
HERRING

DPP EPISODE #19
NICK FROST

DPP EPISODE #66
ADAM BUXTON

DPP EPISODE #37
MICHAEL SMILEY

DPP EPISODE #40
ROMESH RANGAN

E #6
DALM

DPP EPISODE #16

DPP EPISODE #29

DPP EPISODE #9

DISTRACTION PIECES

SCROOBIUS PIP

An Hachette UK Company
www.hachette.co.uk

First published in Great Britain in 2016 by Cassell,
a division of Octopus Publishing Group Ltd
Carmelite House, 50 Victoria Embankment
London EC4Y 0DZ
www.octopusbooks.co.uk
www.octopusbooksusa.com

Distributed in the US by Hachette Book Group
1290 Avenue of the Americas
4th and 5th Floors, New York, NY 10020

Distributed in Canada by Canadian Manda Group
664 Annette St., Toronto, Ontario, Canada M6S 2C8

Commissioning Editor: Hannah Knowles
Editors: Phoebe Morgan & Natalie Bradley
Designer: Jaz Bahra
Typesetter: Ed Pickford
Copy-editor: Susan Pegg
Production Controller: Sarah Kulasek-Boyd

ISBN 978-1-84403-912-8

A CIP catalogue record for this book is available from the British Library

Printed and bound by CPI Group (UK) Ltd, Croydon, CR0 4YY

1 3 5 7 9 10 8 6 4 2

CONTENTS

FOREWORD
by Romesh Ranganathan

Scroobius Pip has always been somebody I have been a fan of and admired; he's fiercely talented and hugely charismatic. I think what draws me to him the most is the fact that every single thing that man does is unadulterated him. He makes no concessions to what is expected of him, and instead allows his instincts to drive him.

It is for this reason that Pip is perfect for the podcast format. The thing that prompts so many of us to make a podcast is that they are so completely liberating and immediate. You figure out what you want to do, you record it, and instantly it is out there for everybody. The podcast world has become densely populated with both mainstream podcasts and condensed radio shows, but also people talking about niche topics and interests passionately. Some podcasts, like *Serial* for example, have taken the format and done something innovative. Others have brought together people with common interests and created communities around them. I have discovered both new interests and new ways of working from listening to various podcasts. I am also spectacularly lazy, and being able to consume something substantial without having to move or even look or concentrate is always going to be appealing.

With so many podcasts out there, it is extremely difficult to mark yourself out as worthy of selection, but *Distraction Pieces* has done that brilliantly. Its primary strength is that Pip is such brilliant company. He's a fascinating conversationalist and I would happily listen to him rabbit on about anything. And he does. Over and above this, however, is his fearlessness in choosing what to talk about and who to talk to. His primary rationale seems to be whatever or whomever he thinks is worthy of discussion, which means that his podcast cannot be defined by any single area. It is delightfully eclectic in its concerns, from discussing football with *Murder in Successville* star Tom Davis, to alopecia and depression with Gail Porter. Pip is fearless in taking the podcast wherever he feels, and that is why *Distraction Pieces* is such a rewarding and varied listen above and beyond almost everything else out there. One minute he will be discussing swearing in West Coast hip-hop, the next he will be discussing the ravages of cancer.

When I guested on one of the early podcasts, I was taken by Pip's interview technique. The man is a stealth Michael Parkinson. I felt very quickly like I was having an effortless chat with a mate, and yet we talked in depth and at length about so many topics. In lesser hands, this might have felt laborious, but Pip has a deft touch. One of my favourite episodes is where he talks to rapper Killer Mike. Pip knows exactly where to take the conversation and how to make the chat compelling. Then you listen to the preceding episode and hear Pip doing this just as effectively with Simon Pegg. The man needs his own chat show.

I was so delighted when he told me that he was doing this book. A podcast of such ambition deserves a companion piece of this nature, which pulls out the big themes that keep cropping up throughout the podcast interviews, and curates them into an engaging and fascinating read – with added bits of Pip to boot. I cannot wait for you to read it. Obviously, skip to my bit first then check out the other shit later.

**Romesh Ranganathan
June 2016**

INTRODUCTION

SCROOBIUS PIP
DISTRACTION PIECES

Good lord, I fucking LOVE podcasts. And it's not just because I have one. My love for podcasts started way before that...

In April 2014, after just over a year of hosting a hip-hop and spoken word radio show on Xfm (now Radio X), my producer, Dan Riedo, and I unexpectedly won two Radio Academy Awards. The very next morning, slightly hungover from the festivities, I set off on my second holiday in seven years, which consisted of driving around and exploring a good portion of France. That journey was largely soundtracked by podcasts. Not radio shows or podcasts of radio shows, but podcasts. It was around this point that I started to toy with the idea that podcasting was what I wanted to pour my time and efforts into.

In 2013 I was lucky enough to be a guest on one of my favourite podcasts, *The Joe Rogan Experience*, and when discussing my radio show I realized I couldn't really give a good reason as to why I worked for someone else. Don't get me wrong, I LOVE Xfm. From the very start of my music career it has been one of my most important supporters, and if Eddy Temple-Morris, Chris Baughen, the Managing Editor of Xfm, and Dan Riedo hadn't talked me into starting the Beatdown then *Distraction Pieces* MAY never have happened. But... my show was on at midnight on a Saturday night. And it was there for a reason. When given options of time slots, I chose the one that would come under the least scrutiny. As elitist as it sounds, I didn't really want passers-by tuning in – at the risk of my offending them or getting complaints for some of the subjects covered and the show's content. I wanted to be buried in the night schedule where those who were tuning in were tuning in specifically for our show. And, with that in mind, it became more and more apparent that it wasn't THAT important where that show was located.

After some long discussions with the team at Xfm it was agreed that, on the commercial side of things, we weren't really bringing in the numbers. With my tastes drifting over to the world of podcasting (a world I was convinced was about to blow up in the UK), it was the perfect time to part ways, leaving the Beatdown as the beautiful little creation we wanted it to be and not having to compromise it in the name of ratings or time delegation.

So I set about planning *Distraction Pieces* and what I wanted it to be.

For me, podcasts had started in the UK with *The Ricky Gervais Show* and the *Adam and Joe* podcasts. But after that boom they seemed to have eased off a little. My focus had certainly drifted to content coming out of the US. Podcasts like the *The Joe Rogan Experience* and *WTF with Marc Maron* provide hours and hours of conversation and entertainment every week. And they do so on their own terms.

And that part is VERY important to me.

It's the whole point of 'Now it's Your Turn' on page 214 (in which I lay down some very basic guidelines as to how YOU can start your own podcast). At a time when mass media had become a smoke show of hidden agendas by dusty backbenchers, podcasts suddenly seemed to appear and offer uncensored secret-agenda-free broadcasts. That's not to say they don't have agendas, but simply that the agendas are more the views of the individual expressing them than of some background billionaire puppet master.

Podcasts suddenly represented free media in every sense of the word. They were shows on which you could be free to express what you wanted, how you wanted and, equally as importantly, they were free for the listeners. They were even free from the schedule restrictions of radio's 'tonight at nine we will be discussing...' traditions. Podcasts were yours to listen to when you wanted, where you wanted. And that excited me hugely.

So I started making a list of people I had come into contact with and could even, possibly, maybe, be bold enough to call 'friends' over my eight or so years as a touring musician. I then contacted them and set out to record a few episodes.

When I launched I wanted to have a few podcasts already in the bag so that I could start strong. I feel one of the keys to a podcast growing is consistency; your listeners knowing that every Wednesday (in our case) there WILL be a new podcast for your trip to work or your evening jog. I also had to figure out what I wanted the podcast to be. So much of our modern media and entertainment has been broken down into 'digestable chunks', and I thought that was assuming too little of people. I decided I wanted the podcast to be 60–90 minutes of unedited discussion. I figured that, even if it put some people off, there WERE people out there who still had the attention span to handle such a daunting engagement.

After making a long list and starting to contact a few people, I decided on my first four interviewees: Russell Brand, Zane Lowe, Alan Moore and DJ Yoda. This, off the bat, felt like a nice statement of intent. A range of names from a variety of lines of work – some of whom had been discussed in great depth already, others curiously unexplored by mainstream media.

This seemed like a solid start and the reaction when they dropped proved that to be an understatement. Now, to be clear, I didn't really know what I was doing.

Worgie (Warren Borg) was my closest audio-type friend so he helped me to put the podcasts together. Then, having helped a little with my website in the past, Jarrod and Steve at BSI Merch helped me get them online and hosted (until I found my way to Acast, who will be covered in 'Now it's Your Turn'). It was a bumbling, cobbled-together mess... but it worked.

Before we knew it the *Distraction Pieces* podcast was in the top ten podcasts in the UK on iTunes. We went on to climb to the number one spot, getting praise from the *Guardian*, *Buzzfeed*, *Shortlist*, the *AV Club* and many more esteemed areas of paper and Internet-based real estate.

There have been guests and episodes along the journey that have knocked me off my feet and made me genuinely feel part of something important, and there have been episodes and guests that have made me wonder how we haven't put off or offended our whole audience by now. Throughout this book I will go into a few of those in a little more detail and, more importantly, let their words and views be documented here for you all to take in and enjoy.

The idea of a book simply transcribing what is already free and forever available in cyberspace seemed pointless to me. But the opportunity to discuss further some of the topics and to highlight some of the amazing insights I have been lucky enough to have shared with my guests has me typing away right now with the drive and excitement of someone who, quite frankly, just wants to finish this so I can take it all in and experience it again myself.

Scroobius Pip
June 2016

1

COMEDY AND THE MOVIES

Music is obviously one of my three main loves; the other two are cinema and stand-up comedy. I am a firm believer that both TV and cinema have come a long, long way since being mockingly referred to as 'the idiot box'. I have made connections with characters in TV and film that were as great as any I have made with characters in literature. Documentaries and non-fiction shows have educated me as much as any textbook or teacher. The range of subjects covered and available for you to consume in this sensory-stimulating manner is almost endless.

I still go to the cinema several times a month, as I truly love the experience of being immersed in film. At home there will always be distractions while you are watching TV, as you glance at your phone or look over at the pile of washing you are yet to deal with, but, in there, it's just you and the piece of art in front of you. Darkness all around you and sound coming from every direction.

I don't go to the cinema to escape reality, quite the opposite – I go to the cinema to enhance my own reality. To be inspired and to feel a whole range of emotions.

Comedy is similar for me in that way. Over the years stand-up has become so wide in style and subject matter that it, too, can be a great learning tool as well as an amazing source of entertainment. People like Lenny Bruce, Stewart Lee, Joe Rogan, Doug Stanhope and Anthony Jeselnik have genuinely opened my eyes to different outlooks on life while simultaneously making sure that those very same eyes are dispensing tears of laughter at a steady rate.

Whether for the views, for the art, or for the sheer entertainment, I pray that movies and comedy will always be as big a part of my life as they are now.

ADAM BUXTON

Where comedy meets music

Or, just add a Muppet

AB: The things that stick out from growing up in South Wales are listening to the radio and taping things off the radio, which in those days meant I'd get my dad's dictaphone and stick it in front of the radio. I'd do a few links and pretend I had my own radio show: 'Coming up next, here's one from Terry Wogan... This is "The Floral Dance".' I remember thinking, I like 'The Floral Dance'; it's amusing.

And I liked *The Muppet Show*, and the songs they had on that – obviously 'Mahna Mahna', which still bears listening to today. And I even had the *Muppet* cast album, and there were a lot of good songs on there. They did a funny cover of 'Tenderly', a smooch MOR [middle of the road] track. It was Animal doing it, so it was all crazy and psychedelic rock. The musicianship on some of those records was brilliant.

SP: *It was a stroke of genius having the Flight of the Conchords guys on to write the songs for the new film [released in 2011]. That's the perfect match for the Muppets: instantly the songs were hilarious.*

AB: Jemaine and Bret from the Conchords are, I think, as good as comedy musicians have ever been. I can't really think of too many people who've been as good as they are. Their songs are genuinely catchy, the lyrics are memorable and clever and have some emotional heft as well as comedy chops. There's a song called 'Carol Brown' that brings a tear to my eye. That's a good song. There are few comedy songs you can bear to hear more than a few times. Even 'Gangnam Style' palls after 5,000 plays, but the Conchords are still amazing.

I've always loved the Muppets. They were my entry into a lot of music. They used to cover a lot of obscure songs from other eras that perhaps *The Muppet Show* viewers wouldn't be familiar with, and revitalized them, reinvented them.

SP: *But with the addition of a Muppet. I've always said that most computer games can be improved with the addition of Mario, or a Mario Brother. It's the same with the Muppets: take a good song, add a Muppet. Do you prefer the Muppet version or the Van Morrison version of 'Bein' Green'?*

AB: They're both quite different. Probably the Muppets' one. Yeah. It's kind of a cheesy song really, and when Van does it it's one of his cheesier songs. Still a great song and I still love it, and it's very jazzy and breezy, but it's maybe a little too Radio 2, if you know what I mean? No disrespect, obviously, to Radio 2, but maybe Kermit has the edge on that one. And thereafter I always liked funny and silly songs.

ADAM BUXTON, cont'd

Saturday night silliness

Or, being weird and marginal

SP: *What drew you to comedy? The beauty of* The Adam and Joe Show *– I remember watching it on Channel 4 when it came out; it felt like mates messing about, and the beauty there is that there doesn't need to be an influence, in a way. Just being silly with your mates is what that show encapsulated.*

AB: I liked broad silly stuff. Joe and I were wary of taking ourselves too seriously and being too up ourselves, even though we were pretty up ourselves. And at that point, when we were doing *The Adam and Joe Show*, we both had been exposed to very finely wrought, brilliant comedy. Things like *Larry Sanders* and *Seinfeld*. Then in the UK, things that Chris Morris and Armando Iannucci were doing, and we really loved those. And I suppose we wanted to emulate those in some way or at least do our version of those kinds of things. A very twisted version. And I mean twisted as in bent, not dark, because our stuff wasn't dark or strange, it was silly, because we both liked silly things.

I can't speak for Joe, but I certainly grew up watching a lot of Saturday-night stuff – *Cannon and Ball.* I didn't love *Cannon and Ball* but I would watch that stuff, and *Crackerjack,* and things like that. I found a lot of those kinds of shows fairly annoying.

And similarly, Russ Abbot, although I must say I did find a lot of Russ Abbot's stuff very funny. He just made me chuckle, he was just a funny person. And he was just a silly character. His support network as well – Bella Emberg and Dustin Gee and Les Dennis. A pretty talented lot of people there, I'd say, on Russ Abbot's show.

Kelly Monteith's show was one of the first shows that I was aware of that broke the fourth wall. It was pretty broad, quite crass, sometimes quite sexist stuff that he would do on there – little observational riffs. But it was quite ahead of its time because he would basically be delivering a stand-up set but they would film it as if it was a narrative sitcom. So he'd be in a hotel room and they'd do a little bit to camera about stuff that happens in hotel rooms, and then he'd walk out and join a conference or something in the hotel, maybe interact with some characters wandering around there, but he'd be continuing to deliver his set to the camera. So you'd be, 'Woah, this feels like a sitcom but he's talking to the camera, this is weird.'

There was still that idea when I started out that 'proper comedy' was made by professionals in studios with big budgets and big personalities and proper equipment. You can't just have fucking twats with video cameras pissing about. That's not TV, that's a weird marginal sideshow. But the nice thing about being weird and marginal is that no one really bothers you; you can do whatever you like.

JOSIE LONG

Gender isn't a genre

Or, my womanhood does not influence my abilities

SP: *I wanted to discuss [Andrew Lawrence's statement] that the quota filling of panel shows, having to have a female comedian on each week, has meant that rather than having on the best comedians, they always have essentially any female comedian and, his argument was, it doesn't give a good representation of female comedians because often it's female comedians who haven't found themselves yet.*

JL: I think he can go fuck himself for saying that. Firstly, if you've got a panel show where a man is the boss, where two older men are the team captains and a man is the boss, no matter how generous they try to be there's already an atmosphere where it's a male-controlled thing...

I don't view men and women in categorical terms like this, but, in my experience, sometimes with certain shows, you go on them, the crowd doesn't know you because you're not famous. As a woman, quite often, women are systematically denied the career-advancing opportunities of their male peers, right? So they're not given their own TV show necessarily, they're not given the big sell-out tours, they're not pushed in the same way. So then what happens is they're all at level one, the men got to level three, the women aren't given that chance to go up to level three. So then the men are on level-three fame, and the people in the crowd – people who've gone for free audience tickets for something, who are quite conservative anyway – they recognize the men, so they trust the men and they laugh at the men. They don't recognize the women, they already have conservative attitudes toward women, so then they don't laugh at the women, the women have a harder time. It's hard, right? There are bullies on them... It's a really wide thing about comedy in general.

SP: *It's such a tough thing to judge as well because of the editing in those shows.*

JL: There are lots of problems and factors.

SP: *When he [Lawrence] said that, I had watched a show that week where one of the comedians I didn't think particularly nailed it on the show was female, and it made me start to go, 'Well, what is that?' But I also thought that when I saw him (and again, I'm saying this having previously seen one really good set from Andrew Lawrence) on* Live at the Apollo *and it wasn't very good. Editing can cause that, but it made me realize that, hang on, I'm now analysing this on the fact that it's a woman, and remembering that the woman wasn't funny rather than remembering someone wasn't funny.*

JL: Yes! This is it, right? The first thing I would desperately want to say is, over and over again, gender isn't a genre, gender isn't a genre. It doesn't fucking matter; like, my womanhood does not influence my abilities. The fact that there's still anyone in this country able to voice the opinion 'women aren't funny' is a fucking travesty because it's meaningless. Women are 51 per cent of the population, it means fuck all, and to say, 'Oh, women comedians...' That annoys me.

SP: *Completely. One of the biggest arguments I've had when posting about this podcast is that I always say, 'Bring your suggestions of who you'd like to be on,' and I end up arguing with people when they say, 'I'd like to hear some women,' and I think that's the wrong request. I feel you should request specific women that you'd like because otherwise it's kind of... I don't know. I find that blanket 'I'd like to hear some women...' Who? Which women? I don't book this based on gender. I book it based on, oh, this will be a fascinating conversation and there's loads of women I'd like to have on and I'd like for people to request them, but you don't have people saying, 'I'd like to hear some men,' or, 'I'd like to hear...' Do you know what I mean?*

JL: Well, it's tricky, it's very tricky, because I'm all for quotas and there being more, because we should just be better represented, right?

It should just be that you see about half as many women as you do men in your TV culture, because that's just how many of us there are.

The problem is it's not like that, and the problem is all of us, I think, have to be quite aggressive in our heads, trying to even up the score.

Take my podcast with Robin Ince: I'd always thought, well, it is an equally represented podcast because the hosts are a man and a woman, but then obviously if all the guests are men, it's not. I do think we have a responsibility to go out of our way to put an equal amount of men and women on, even though that is in a way generalizing and tokenizing. It's the same with representing people of BAME [black, Asian and minority ethnic] backgrounds, representing people of all ethnicities.

SP: *I guess everyone has to have that kind of responsibility. It still freaks me out to think that I will ever sit down and think, right, I probably need to get three more women, an Asian guy... I really don't want to think like that because then it's bringing race and gender into decisions where I haven't got that, but maybe I have to have it, because other people have it in a negative way, so... When all the Ferguson stuff was happening, one of the best quotes I saw was: 'It's not enough as a white person to be not racist any more.' That's not enough, you need to be active.*

JL: You have to try to change society.

SP: *Yeah, to change it, because as white people with all the privilege we've got and the way things are at the moment, just simply not being racist isn't enough.*

JL: Because the problem's still happening. But I tell you the other thing as well, sort of back to Andrew Lawrence slagging off women on panel shows. There was definitely an era, that I think we're coming to the end of, where on a panel show you'd have male comedians and then a female model or presenter, and that really upset me because I'd be like, 'They're stealing our jobs! There's that woman who's taken my job!' But we're not in that era any more; things are changing.

SP: *It's great and odd that it all seems to be coming together at once, almost. As we were just talking of panel shows, it's not one woman that* *happens to be going on and doing it... A while back it seemed Sarah Millican was the female comedian: she's great, she's huge, she's wonderful, but that was it.*

JL: They let one get through!

SP: *Yes, exactly that. But it seems in 2014 I saw comedian after comedian, including ones I hadn't heard of, and it becoming the norm of it not being a thing of male or female.*

JL: It's the normalizing of it. It feels like things are changing for the better. It feels like there's more acceptance again. Maybe the nineties and the start of the two thousands there was a real backlash against the eighties. Because you look at 1985 onwards – Victoria Wood, French and Saunders – some of the most successful comedians that existed were female. Maybe I'm rose-tinting it, but, for example, *Roseanne* was the biggest show in America then. It almost felt like there was a backlash afterwards. But lately it's just felt really exciting. America's so helpful because, like, *Girls* has been so big. Amy Poehler, Tina Fey, all of these are massive cultural comedic icons, you know? So I do feel very positive.

SARA PASCOE

I don't represent my gender

Or, I can't help this is the life I've lived

SP: *There has been a lot of talk in the last couple of years about women on panel shows.*

SPa: It's a really odd thing: although I knew I was a girl, I didn't identify as a woman until doing comedy, when people just tell you about it all the time. I've always felt like a person. I didn't feel I was girly or boyish.

I always felt like a human being. Which is a really good sign of not having ever felt oppressed, I guess.

SP: *This is a really bad thing to liken that to but I've had that with being tall. I never knew I was tall until I started getting known and everyone now going, 'Oh you're taller than I expected.' I now think of myself as a tall person, whereas I've not grown.*

SPa: It's not self-imposed; it's not how you identify until other people do. So then I guess you do have a heightened awareness of it. The only difficulty is that with any types of creativity it comes back to that failure thing. You've got to be allowed to be shit, to make stuff. You've got to be allowed to be messy or clumsy, because you're trying to get at something. If there's part of you that thinks you're representing your race or the country you come from, or your gender, the danger is that the responsibility you feel makes you think you can't be bad.

How panel shows tend to work is you do lots of warm-ups for them – as in a dry run through so no one films it. It's like an audition – they'll use less famous comedians. It's a safe area. I really thought I wanted to do panel shows, and I'm not doing them as a woman. If I'm shit on them it's because I'm shit. If I'm bad on them, I'm never representing my gender, because I can't and that's not my responsibility. If someone else says, 'She's shit, just like all women,' then they were going to think that anyway.

SP: *They had a predisposed opinion.*

SPa: Exactly. And as we know, they can be strengthened and reinforced by evidence that seems to support it, or what tends to happen is people go, 'I hate when people say women aren't funny: Tina Fey's funny.' Finding exceptions to a rule reinforces the rule. So I try just as much as possible not to engage with it. If I'm having a bad show I don't think, oh you should probably say something or there's probably going to be some fat bald middle-aged man sitting at home going, 'See, they're all shit.' Well, fine, let him think that.

I once got in a taxi and I was talking to the taxi driver about books and he said he didn't read books by women because they weren't as well researched. And that for me encapsulates the people who say women aren't funny. There's no point arguing with that man. If I'd recommended *Wolf Hall* to him as a book, he would see that either as an exception or he'd just disbelieve me. So I asked him about what he liked and he liked Andy McNab books and I realized that's fine, because he's finding pleasure in something and me getting angry with him in a car is going to make him think I'm mad rather than that he's wrong.

SP: *But what a bizarre specific thing to think.*

SPa: That's how it feels to me whenever someone says something to me about women in comedy. Or women in their lives. If someone's wife doesn't make them crack up or their sisters or their friends, that's a bit of a sad life.

All stand-up is really authored, as in it's all about your experiences. But as women, when we talk about our experiences it's seen as feminist, rather than 'I can't help this is the life I've lived'. I wear skirts sometimes and I've got long hair, so that means it's feminist? Because men are the norm. That's the odd thing. Being a subculture when you're over half a society. But anyway, it's a fascinating time we live in.

RICHARD HERRING

Defining success

Or, is the prize worth the winning?

RH: Throughout my twenties I was on TV but I was pretty much staying at home playing *Civilization II* on my computer all weekend because I was too scared to ring anyone and say, 'Do you want to come out?'

SP: *There are achievements there; they're just not real-world achievements...*

RH: So when people go, 'Oh, it must have been amazing...' Seriously, we hardly went to any parties and, though there were lots of good things, I have to say, I was very shy and very self-conscious.

I'm really content with who I am now, and where I am. And I think for a long time I wasn't. I was either wanting to be more recognized, or more famous or more successful. I'm really glad none of that happened... I think with the Lee & Herring thing, I'd have loved being famous and marrying a supermodel and all that stuff: I'm so glad I didn't go down that route. I think it would have driven me mad. If Lee & Herring had been *Little Britain* (I don't know why that came to mind!), then I think it would have destroyed us both. I think Stewart wouldn't have liked being that popular and I would have gone nuts the other way.

SP: *Thank God for* Civilization *keeping you in.*

RH: Well, I was very unlikely to meet a supermodel with the lifestyle I had. I can't believe I've been depressed in my life because I've had a very lucky life, and I've worked for 25 years and always worked, and I can't imagine there isn't something for me to do for the next 20 years; even if it isn't performing, even if it's just producing, or pole dancing or whatever.

SP: *It's an interesting industry. I was discussing this with Kurt Sutter, who wrote* Sons of Anarchy *and* The Shield *and stuff like that. And it's a fascinating industry because in entertainment you'll see the movies and think 'I love movies, I wanna be a movie star,' and you forget there are a million other roles that are part of that as well. As soon as you've been at the front, you forget you've got all this experience. So if there is a point where you feel you're done with being on stage, you've had so many years of the tour management side of it and everything else... But it's that constantly scary thing – it's not a job where you've got your pension or everything else all stacked up.*

RH: What's nice is I do feel content and I don't feel bitter about anything, most of the time. I'm not looking at other people going, 'Argh, I wish that was me.' I genuinely look at Stew and I'm delighted for him.

Because I think he deserves it. And I think people would expect me not to be... And I think also it gives you hope that that can happen. So there are lots of positives. I mean, it could have happened to a nicer person, but there are lots of positives.

SP: *It literally could have happened to a nicer person.*

RH: And also, it's whether you want that. There's a quote in *Vanity Fair*, which I studied at A level. Dobbin, this character, spends his whole life trying to court this woman and eventually marries her and it's not that good. There's a line saying that the prize he'd spent his life trying to get wasn't worth the winning. I sort of think, the thing that I would have aspired to and wanted from this, I would have hated and it would have destroyed me. And what I've got is much more valuable and much more enjoyable.

ROMESH RANGANATHAN

Finding your feet

Or, delivering the worst set of comedy that has ever been

SP: *So how did you start off in comedy? You failed miserably in a rap battle final; you were a maths teacher for a while... What was the process?*

RR: The first time I did a gig I was about nine years old. We'd gone to a Pontins camp and they had a talent competition and I entered. Two things I did: one, I did it in a Sri Lankan accent – I thought that would add to the humour of it – and secondly, it was mainly material I'd got from *3001 Jokes*, which was a book I'd got at the time. There are a lot of anti-Irish jokes from books when I was growing up. So it was a combination of a kid doing a Sri Lankan accent and doing loads of racist anti-Irish jokes.

SP: *And you didn't give up?*

RR: Well, I did give up for a long time. I was happily teaching and I'd watched so much stand-up and been so obsessed with it and thought it was something to do as a bucket list thing, so I blagged my way on to a gig. I was a comedy fan who had no appreciation for the craft at all. Comedy, when it's done well, looks so easy. And I fell into the trap – as everyone does, I think – of going, 'Oh, I'm funny. I'll put this thing together.' And I went to the Comedy Café in Shoreditch and delivered what was probably the worst set of comedy that has ever been. I'd think worldwide. I died on my arse, you'd be happy to hear. But I liked it.

It takes so long to be yourself on stage. I didn't think about what style I was going to have, I just thought about the material, and how the way you deliver stuff is so important. Your performance is so important. And it wasn't a conscious thing.

When I started doing open mic stuff I definitely went through a process where, if you saw me six months in, I was more deadpan – there was no performance at all. Then I went through a stage of just being a bit more needy. These weren't deliberate strategies. You're looking for the laugh so your brain is going, 'Try this.' I wasn't thinking, 'Today I'll try this.'

But eventually who you are offstage and who you are onstage just gets closer and closer together, but you have to get the chops. You have funny ideas but stand-up is almost like a different language. And I'm still not the stand-up I want to be. You don't have the ability to express yourself; you're a version of yourself.

And eventually, as you get better or more experienced, you'll have an idea offstage and can translate it quicker into something the audience will get on board with. You've got to be so attuned to how to deliver something to an audience. You can say harsh things if you want but the audience has to understand your logic. Which is why when you see inexperienced comics – who will see someone like Frankie Boyle who says some pretty offensive things – they'll think, 'Oh, I'm going to say something full on,' but they haven't got the skills to deliver that in a way that's not going to turn everyone off.

I don't know if it's that with comedy: that if people don't like it, they hate it. If they hate it, they want that person to die.

SP: *I appreciate highbrow humour, but it doesn't have to be. It can just be funny. People falling over is funny.*

RR: You can fall victim to being a snob about it. I love comedy that's highbrow and makes you think, but I've never gone to a show where somebody's talked about nothing for an hour, laughed my head off, then come out and said, 'But what's he actually saying about the world?' I just think entertaining is entertaining. And if someone entertains you and they say something that's great. However, I'd be much more pissed off if I went to a stand-up show and I learned something and it wasn't funny than if it was hilarious and I didn't learn anything about myself or the human condition. I don't give a shit about that. It's just funny.

ROMESH RANGANATHAN, cont'd

Rapping comedians and funny rappers

Or, transferable skills

SP: *Was rapping a lead into comedy? A lot of battling is insults and the people who genuinely win the freestyle are the ones with the best punchlines. I always remember watching Scribble Jam, and there'd be some guys doing the most amazing stuff, but then other guys would come out with punchline after punchline and steal the show.*

RR: They do a comedians' rap battle in Edinburgh and I was up against Carl Donnelly. What he was saying was so much more interesting than what I was saying; he had nice little twists and word play, and I just talked about his mum.

And I said to him afterwards, what you did was loads better than what I did, but it's something visceral the audience can grab on to. If you just say something horrible, like a punchline, and the audience lap it up.

Donnelly and I spoke to each other on the phone before it and said we'll agree there's no limit. I wasn't reading reviews, and Donnelly found a two-star review of me and started quoting it as part of his rap. It was brutal.

I entered a freestyle competition. It was pre-Jump Off; it was called Battle Scars. You had to send in a little snippit of a verse, then they'd select people and then they did a big gig at Scala in King's Cross in front of judges. I'll be honest with you: mixed results.

SP: *It's changed a lot now; it's not really freestyling. You get months to prepare and I've got mixed feelings about that. I loved Scribble Jam and stuff like that, but the reality is the standard is going to be higher if you've all had some time to prepare. But you're not then going to get that buzz when a line is really killer.*

RR: It's like when you watch a comedian go into a crowd and riff on something, the response that gets is 'Bam!' It's so exciting to watch a comic leave their set and just go off. And that's the thing that you're losing with that. You get better-constructed stuff and it all ties in, and they've obviously had little Post-its on their turntable going 'I could tie that lyric up with this', so the standard is good but you don't get that buzz.

I'm not taking anything away from it because I think they're really talented, but as a spectacle I don't enjoy it as much as I used to. When someone references something, or something happens in the room there and then, it's so exciting.

I think there are a lot of transferable skills between live music and stand-up. I've watched so much live music and as a comedian you are working off the energy of the crowd. If a crowd's good and you tune into what they like, or you tune into their energy, the show becomes so much better and you enjoy yourself more and they enjoy themselves more.

With hip-hop, there's loads of really funny hip-hop rappers – they've got such great senses of humour. A lot of it is just really funny observations, like stand-up. You listen to it and think, this guy's really hilarious; it just happens to rhyme. I don't know if you ever listened to *Kwest Tha Madd Lad*? It's one of the funniest albums I've ever heard and I remember listening to his turn of phrase and thinking he could easily be a comedian. Comedy and hip-hop go hand in hand: there's so much that crosses over.

SARA PASCOE

Comedy is not bourgeois

Or, occasionally you have to deal
with customer feedback

SPa: I did stand-up as an experiment after breaking up with a boy-friend. It's perfect when you're broken up. You have all this hot energy, you just do stuff; you usually make stuff. So stand-up is great. You can write new stuff every day. You can talk about the person that's hurt you as well. And people love pain.

In the honeymoon period of it I just couldn't believe this thing existed. And I didn't think about career, or money, or job. The surprise to me now is the fact I pay my rent from stand-up, the fact I don't have a proper job. That's what I kind of work out: how much longer I've got before I'd have to temp again. I'd still carry on doing stand-up for nothing. What I really respect is the form of it. It felt like a proper craft, where you were never going to be good enough – you could always be that slight bit better.

SP: *Stewart Lee is one I often use to show people how crafted it can be. Just because his stuff is so intricate. That has to have been written down, and referenced, and moved around to work.*

SPa: For some people the craft goes into making it look like they've just thought of it. And they're talking just like a person talks when they've had an idea, so the craft is all completely hidden. Stewart – and he would say this – he writes it using words like notes in jazz, as motifs. So certain words have importance or are stressed at certain points. There are patterns that are then broken and you're able to enjoy that as well as the content.

SP: *When you write, how much of it is finding a funny idea and how much is 'I've got a message to put across'?*

SPa: It comes from both things: the beautiful thing about Edinburgh Fringe is you have a really long time to work it out. With an Edinburgh show you don't have to go, 'Well I don't know what's funny about that yet.'

SP: *That's got to be a great motivation in itself, to have those things that you're like, 'I know there's something there – at some point I'll be able to get to that.'*

SPa: That's the beauty of this job – it's just about communication. Sometimes I can communicate exactly what I want; other times I'm still too messy with something so I need to work out exactly what I feel and how to present that, which isn't telling people what to think. I hate when people preach, especially comedians, because I think: you're one of life's clowns, you're one of life's losers, do not tell me how to live my life.

SP: *Yes, I think that is one of the most underrated traits in a person is the ability to say, 'I'm wrong,' or, 'I don't understand this.' Because I think so many people don't have that. It took me a while, but now I love to learn I'm wrong.*

SPa: One of the first things you have to learn if you're going to do any kind of public performance is you're not going to be liked by everyone. The thing that is so horrible at school, the thing that feels so horrible growing up, that you can't please everyone, then becomes a fact of your life. That in any room, a percentage of people think you're doing your job badly, should not be allowed to do your job, or just technically, with comedy, 'That's not comedy.' Actually undermine it: 'You didn't do comedy there because I didn't laugh.'

SP: *The slogan of my record label is: 'We may not be for you and that's fine.' Because I think that is just the best thing to live by.*

SPa: I remember growing up, people saying Coldplay are shit and me going, 'Did they not learn to play their instruments? Did they not turn up to their gig on time?' I think that's the thing I had to stop me becoming too anxious about work – if they don't laugh, as long as I've done my time, and I did my best, I'm still allowed to call that an achievement: I didn't turn up really drunk, I didn't not turn up.

SP: *I remember a stand-up explaining to the crowd that they have been to far more comedy stand-up gigs than the crowd have so they had to trust that this is funny – 'I guarantee you, this is amusing and entertaining.'*

SPa: Stewart Lee once got heckled in Edinburgh and he is the perfect example of how to deal with it. Someone shouted out, 'You're not funny,' and he said, 'No, *you* don't think I'm funny.' Some people think I'm funny, some people here might think I'm funny, people at other gigs might think I'm funny, some people never think I'm funny. You are absolutely entitled to not enjoy this and that's fine.

What I love about comedy is that it's classless and that it's not bourgeois. People can tell you they hate you, they can get up and leave or they can just go to the bar – they can do it in polite ways or they can do it in rude ways. But I love that no one ever feels oppressed. Even though you've got a microphone, they know that part of your job is occasionally having to deal with customer feedback. Although it can be horrible it is important that that never stops.

RUFUS HOUND

Getting into comedy and staying there

Or, just start

SP: *I'd imagine there is a long journey of getting into the comedy world, and getting accepted and graduating through the ranks.*

RH: I had some really good advice from Ross Noble's manager before I'd ever done stand-up, because I was saying to him, 'I've been thinking maybe I might...' And he said, 'Look, here's the thing, right.

Just start. Just starting is hard enough, so before you've got any plan or whatever, just start. Then, get good. That's going to take some time: just getting the stage time to get good is going to be hard. You don't even know if you can do it until you've done a hundred gigs, so you need to get to your hundred-gig point. Then assess, is this something you're going to do? Then once you're getting paid; once you're doing the opening set for 25 quid or whatever at all these open mic spots, which should be the first time you ever approach a proper club that's offering proper money. And you're certainly not asking them for money, you're just asking for an open spot, ten minutes. You've got to have a really good 20 minutes that you've built up over the open mic spot before you're then going to go and do a free ten minutes at any club worth its salt. And it's like that thing of: do your tour, record the DVD, sell that DVD on the next tour... Every stage, it's like you get further ahead then sell it backwards. So then be in the clubs and say, well, I'll work for free here, but I'll demand to get paid there because that's a better club than that club. And that's how you build it all up.'

SP: *It's good to know the systems and pecking order and how that would run. That advice sounds quite simple and almost like he was trying to put you off, because it's essentially saying, this has to be a passion project because it might only ever be a passion project. But that's valuable information, to know how the climb is. And particularly these days, in a world where comedy is selling out the O2 [arena] and venues like that, so people look at that and go, 'I'd like to do that.' Well, would you? Would you be willing to commit, you know, ten years of your life to get to that stage, or do you want essentially a kickstarter campaign to say, 'You provide me with those ten years and I'll jump straight in at the fun bit.'*

RH: It's funny that you say now that comedy is selling out at the O2, because what it's done: it's made people think about doing stand-up who would never previously have thought of doing it. Now it feels like, oh, you could be a rock star comic if you wanted to be. There had been a few rock star comics: Newman and Baddiel had sold out Wembley Arena. But when I started doing it, Eddie Izzard had put videos out, and he'd sold a few videos, but no one else was really buying home recordings of stand-up shows. A few were, a rarefied few.

SP: *At that point it was more about going to comedy clubs, rather than comedy gigs, so rather than going to see Eddie Izzard, you're going to see some stand-up.*

RH: That was exactly it. You could earn a very good living just doing 20 minutes in a club. You know, in London you could maybe squeeze two or three gigs in together, or you'd be a bit further out of town, but the money was good. You could earn a living doing it. That money hasn't changed in the last 20 years, because more people have come in. There have been more clubs, more open mics, so the money's got spread out, but no one's getting paid more than they were 20 years ago.

SP: *I still find it amazing and inspiring to see the general work ethic or mindset of a stand-up – trying to get a few sets in one night.*

RH: It's like that old story of the car pulling up alongside a famous musician or conductor – depending on which version you hear – and this guy looks out, has no idea who he is and says to him, 'Excuse me, sir, do you know the way to Carnegie Hall?' He says, 'Practice.'

STEWART LEE

Stand-up is enough

Or, do nothing except this, then die

SP: *The thing I find beautiful about your TV show is that it is essentially doing what you've always been doing. That's so rare. Even for a lot of the greats in stand-up, stand-up seems to be a stepping-stone rather than, 'Here's what I want to do.' There are few examples of people having* *a high-level long career, rather than that they have their career as a stand-up, then get into acting or writing TV shows or films.*

SL: A lot of things in people's lives, which look like moral or artistic choices, are just about what they can cope with. I'm not very good at ceding responsibility for things. I'm not very good at cooperating.

SP: *So one-man stand-up is perfect for you?*

SL: In the past I had developed other projects. Like *Jerry Springer: The Opera* – I worked with Richard Thomas, the composer, on that. We worked on it unpaid for three years then, when it finally did get into a commercial space, we couldn't really get paid for it anyway. I'd never have the time or freedom financially to work on something for nothing now. I've got the kids and I have to juggle things around with the wife.

The thing about stand-up is you can get on with it at your own pace. If you have an idea, you will eventually be able to do it somewhere because all you need is a mic and a room. So it's free of overheads. And also, when I was lucky enough to get asked to work on the opera – this is 15 years ago now, 2001 – after 12, 13 years of doing stand-up I thought, at last, a big canvas.

So we did all that, then at the end of it we got into loads of trouble for it. We couldn't get paid. And also, if you did want to make a change to something, the machinery of a big show was so vast, you'd have got the band of ten people, cast of forty, everyone had to be cut in. Even a line change would have repercussions. Then I thought, well, stand-up. Plus there's the fact that I've got paid more doing a show for 50 people in a pub than I would have done for the show in a West End theatre because of the overheads and the debt.

Then I suddenly thought, there is nothing I can't do in stand-up. I thought, you can just say it; you can just describe the thing. I don't need to do it in a play. Because I can have sad bits, happy bits, I can have stories. I can act out other people's voices if I want to pretend to have dialogue with people. I can make it like a little story. The long-form shows are like little plays really, in a way. They have a similar plot.

The comedian Stewart Lee – he is a comedian, that's his job and he's trying to do his job. Different things happen but there is a reason for him to be on stage. And I don't think that's over, at all. You can put music in it, if you want. If you keep the music simple – you and one other person – that's not going to break the bank. You could have a little bit of a set, if you want. Most stand-up sets are just their name written in big letters. Whereas when I've done a set it's got some sort of relationship with the material. So if you can get all the set in the van you drive around in as well, brilliant. There's nothing that offers me more creative freedom and nothing makes as much sense, cost effectively, either.

SP: *It's weird because it's the restriction of what you can do that gives the freedom, essentially. We had Alan Moore on the podcast a few months ago and he was saying how the beauty of comics when they first came out, particularly as it was before any CGI or whatever, was that it was the only format in which you could have dragons flying and all these huge things. And that was because of the restriction of it being drawn on paper.*

SL: I wouldn't say it to him but I'll say it to you, that actually his way of thinking about that sort of problem solving has been very influential on me. As a creative thinker I think he's brilliant and I feel very lucky to have got to meet him. He said this great thing once, which is 'don't do anything', basically. Do the thing you want to do and don't make it so expensive that you lose money on it, and don't sign the rights over to someone else.

He said that people kept saying to him, 'Your comic's so good it could be a film.' As if that's the goal. And he said he didn't want it to be a film, he wanted it to be a comic. The opening page of *Watchmen* is written and scripted and directed by a man who has really, really thought about what that medium does. And he's spent his whole life thinking about that. And it is a comic. And it is the best comic of its type. It is not a comic that's auditioning to be a film. It is using how a sequence of drawn images works. And it is much better than the film of *Watchmen* because you don't see what happens between each picture; you have to fill it in in your imagination. In the film, it's made explicit, which doesn't involve you as much. It's not as good.

SP: *The beauty of* Watchmen *– I controversially enjoyed the film, too – but the beauty of the comic was, he made something that couldn't* *be completely accurately turned into a film because of the pages of file notes. It's that true understanding of: this is the medium, this is the beginning and end of it. I'm far more of a fan of spoken word than written poetry. But I understand that in the medium of written poetry there is so much more that can be done than with spoken word, because of the structures.*

SL: And vice versa.

SP: *It's embracing the medium you're in, I guess.*

SL: What I got off Alan Moore is that, actually, I think people feel about stand-up comedy the way they feel about comics: it's a low art form and wouldn't it be great if you could get to do theatre? And wouldn't it be great if you poor little comics who are writing could get to do film? Because film's great, isn't it? There are some fantastic films. There's *Night at the Museum 3*. I think the average film is much worse than the average comic. And I think the average comedian, in the worst highlights on a Saturday night, is better at their job than a lot of actors. Because they have to be, because they're going to be caught out. So I don't see it as a promotion to be told, 'Would you like to come and write a film, would you like to come and do theatre?' Because I can do all those things in stand-up and I can do them with more urgency and drama, and I can get people to listen to the words and think about ideas themselves, and not have to spoon-feed them. And there won't be soundtrack music underneath telling them what feeling they're supposed to have.

SP: *Coldplay. Or Johnny Cash, 'Hurt'.*

SL: Yeah. So my ambition is to do nothing except this, then die. Once you've decided that you don't have to worry about all those other things.

ROBIN INCE

ROBIN INCE

Taking risks

Or, don't ask, 'What does the audience want?'

RI: I've really understood, the older I've got, that anyone who does comedy does it because they must. There are people like Joanna Neary, who's one of my favourite performers, who isn't nearly as popular as she should be – she's proper funny bones. And I'd see all these acts such as hers, and I'd want to put them on. So I started this club called the Book Club and I went on and said, 'Many acts tonight are going to be experimenting, they're going to be doing different things, they're going to be doing things they've never done before. And I think the most important thing for you to know when you're watching them is that sometimes you'll be watching thinking, "Oh I don't really like that," and what you must remember when you have moments like that is to remember that you are wrong.'

Some of the club promoters I knew from years ago, they would watch all the acts. Sometimes they wouldn't book an act that had done really well because they didn't like the cut of their gib or their politics, or something about them, but there was that sense of curation. Then it increasingly seemed to become 'Oh, I'm just outside the door, he's getting big laughs, that's fine.' And it seemed to lose something.

The idea that every time you go for a night out you have to guarantee it's going to work is damaging. As you know, anything that is guaranteed to work night after night after night with no risk whatsoever will ultimately probably be very mundane. If someone starts from that, if their starting point as an artist is 'what does the audience want?' they never break away from it.

SP: *One of the great examples of that is Josie Long – she started at a very early age. I tie you two together because you were someone who provided somewhere for someone like Josie. A lot of comedy at that point was rooted in cynicism and Josie was not that at all. I think over that whole* *time she managed to get about four or five jokes out, the rest was just getting distracted by someone's T-shirt or going off on an excited ramble. Wonderful shows, but it needed a home like that.*

RI: Yes, it's that level of risk taking. The amount of horrible abuse she's had, as well, unfortunately on the Internet, shows that what she does is important and exciting, because people see it as a threat. It's a bit like, I wrote a blog post a while ago and it was about watching Samuel Beckett in Toronto and seeing how cross some people were. You see this apparently disembodied mouth and people are going, 'I don't know what this is at all. What is this? When does it end? What IS this?' He's been dead for 30 years and his work is still so potent that it is celebrated but it's not just become this mundane industry.

RIZ AHMED

Everything is a gift and a curse

Or, no budget is the way to go

SP: *I think a fascinating thing that people won't realize about actors is that physical training can be a part of it. You've said before you've had to train in different ways for different films. Is that something you were aware of before you started, or is it something you've learned off other people as you've got into it?*

RA: I think it's a cultural shift. In Britain, particularly, acting is taught; because Shakespeare is so dominant in our culture, and in drama school acting is taught from a very text-based perspective. All the answers are in the text; they're in the play – if you do your detective work on the text. Rehearsals were often about sitting around a table and talking about it and analyzing stuff. Because that's coming from a theatre point of view – in theatre you get to do the performance once that night. So you're trying to find the optimal way of playing each scene. What is the optimal high stakes way? What is the optimal transaction taking place in this exchange between these two characters? You've got to find that.

SP: *That live and one-off opportunity thing.*

RA: Exactly. So a lot of the focus goes on to text, whereas I feel that in film – and what I've noticed more in the American approach and working more with American directors and actors as well – it's not coming so much from theatre so they don't need to nail that optimal transaction in the same way. It's, 'Let's do the red version of the scene, then the purple one, and a green one, and a black one.' Then the director and the editor can shape it in the edit. So that becomes more about immersing yourself in the character. There's that anecdote with Dustin Hoffman and Laurence Olivier? Was it *Marathon Man* where Dustin Hoffman was running round and round the set trying to make himself out of breath, and Laurence Olivier asked, 'What are you doing?' And he was like, 'I've got to be tired in this scene.' And Olivier said, 'You should try something: it's called acting, darling.'

And there's a different approach sometimes with film and in America with sense memory and method acting that as a British actor I was not exposed to as much. So as I work more in film and as I work more in America I'm being exposed to that and it's interesting. In *Nightcrawler*, for example, we'd sit down for rehearsals: I'd sit down with Jake Gyllenhaal and the director, and I'd be going, 'Yeah, but what do you think is going on here? I think it might be this and this, because if you look at this scene, I say that.' You know, doing that text-based stuff, and Jake would be starving himself. That was his preparation: starving himself. He had a piece of chewing gum and a tea in a day. And I was sitting there thinking, part of me was thinking, what has that got to do with anything? Is this just actor's vanity? But then when we actually got on to set and started doing the scenes, when I saw the film back, I thought, that's kind of genius. This character is desperately hungry, so Jake made himself desperately hungry; it's a different approach.

SP: *People on one side of the fence think that theirs is the right way and the other is the wrong way, and yet it's completely dependent on person-ality – on role even. I remember Morgan Freeman had the same quote* *of 'I don't understand all these method actors: I get up, I act and then I stop acting.' But it's a different thing. It surprised me, because Morgan Freeman was someone I would think of as maybe being into all that. But it's completely individual and personal taste.*

RA: I think it changes day to day and scene to scene: something I'm trying to embrace more and more is accepting that part of any kind of artistic life is about being in a state of confusion. You're not really sure: 'How do you do it? What's your approach?' I don't fucking know, really. I'm not sure. There are some things I will always use as starting points. And a lot of times, if you try to recreate what your process was on the last project, that will hit a brick wall, because it's a different vibe, a different dynamic, a different alchemy between the director and actors on set; the storyline, the pace of shooting. So much of it, I find more and more – and I don't just mean in acting but in making music, in anything, personal relationships – I feel like things have gone better if I just let go a bit more; if I give up on the idea of trying to control it, trying to steer the conversation.

SP: *How was it to go from working in British films – British cinema and TV – to something like* Nightcrawler *that was so LA, so drenched in that feel.*

RA: There are definitely differences. I think there are two kinds of British productions: there's the one that is packaged for a global audience, which is usually big period drama, and they don't cast people like me in that; then there's independent films, and those independent films that I've been proud to be associated with – there's no budget! There's just no budget, everyone is all hands on deck. And I think that's quite good in a way. I enjoy that. I'm someone who doesn't like sitting still and waiting around, and the idea that, 'Right, we have to move at a fast pace – literally all hands on deck. Shit, the floor's wet, it's not meant to be raining in this scene, chuck me a broom.' That's how it was in *Four Lions*, that's how it was in *Shifty*. And I like that: the camaraderie of that. There's a certain pace to that that I like.

It's interesting. When you get more money, then you can take more time. And then there's different kind of gifts that come with that, but also different challenges. Like, you get your time and your space and your headspace – and you get to do your extra take. And they put up extra lighting. Yeah, they've got two cameras, so, wicked, you don't have to repeat it again. But also, maybe, there's the challenge of how do you manage your energy?

SP: *That's an interesting thing you dropped in casually there: how much of a difference it makes when there's two cameras. That sounds like a stupid thing, but until you either make something or analyze a film real-izing that a lot of these scenes are going to have to be done over, and over, and over... Because you're getting the camera close up on you, mid on you, close on the person you're talking to, mid on the two of you talking together. So the fact of having a few of those shots happening at once – that must be kind of amazing, or relieving, to be able to do that. And for the flow of a scene, because you can be more true to keeping more of one actual take rather than piecing together a series of takes.*

RA: It can, it can. But it can also present obstacles. Like, right now, I'm filming this series for HBO called *Criminal Justice*, and some of it takes place in the criminal justice system so it's in prisons and stuff. And prison cells are small, so you're fitting two cameras, with the camera-men, the pullers, the focus and the grips – who are operating the dollies and the tracks that they're on – and the lights that you need to try and nail for both those cameras to get a good angle, and for it to look good in a cell. So that can present a totally different set of obstacles, in a way. Everything is a gift and a curse.

SP: *So that's when it's easier to go back to the low budget.*

RA: It can be.

SP: *Have you come to a point where you have a theory on what actu-ally gets the best end result? I was watching a documentary on Herzog and Kinski at the weekend –* My Best Fiend *– and it was talking a lot about* Aguirre, the Wrath of God, *which is one of my favourite films, and it was revealing that because they were filming it literally on a raft in Peru – a tiny crew – loads of it they literally had one take on. 'Done,* *we're moving on to the next bit.' People are actually going to die getting injured. Serious shit is going down, so they had to film, bang, on to the next bit. I've watched that film loads of times now and been amazed by it, realizing that actually they've not spent days and days crafting that same scene. And I'd imagine that was the same for* Shifty. *That was known for being made on a micro budget, so I'd imagine there was a lot there where you had to get that in the can and move on. Does that pressure get the best out of you, or is having the opportunity to craft and nail it the better option?*

RA: That's a really good question. When you've got no time and no money, there's a high percentage of probability that no one will ever see the film or hear of the film. So the case when those cocktail of ingredients – no time, no budget – the time when that fails is probably quite high. Whereas the big-budget films, you're going to hear about it, regardless. Because they're putting hundreds of millions into making the film and promoting it. So you will see those successes and failures. Whereas with those low-budget successes and failures, if you've heard of the film, if someone has seen the film, then that means it worked. So I guess I'm saying it's a bit of roulette. It can go either way.

But I think there's something about that whole sense of camaraderie and madness and pace of low-budget films that can prevent over-thinking. And things can still feel organic. This is my personal bias; the first film I made was totally improvised – it was that Michael Winterbottom film, *Road to Guantanamo* – and it was just me and three guys, phenomenal actors but who had never acted before, just plucked from colleges in Birmingham. We just went on a road trip through Pakistan and Afghanistan. And Michael was filming us. So all those scenes when we're throwing up, we're really throwing up. We were on this mad Pashtun-like lorry, driving at 80 miles an hour off this cliff, off the Khyber Pass. The drivers over there, a lot of these Pashtun tribesmen come from villages where they just make guns and grow weed. That's all they do. It should be a rap video, really; Pashtun crunk is an untapped genre. So we were going along and I needed to be sick, and there was just one dustbin. And I'm taking a dump in the same dustbin that I'm having to throw up in. And Michael said,

'Let's just get a bit more of a close-up on that.' And I'm just like, 'You're so evil. What are you doing?'

SP: *Fascinating. That way of film-making of really putting people through the situation. Because we're watching it on a screen, it's fine. It's putting people through those trials and you get something amazing.*

RA: But that was my first experience, so in a way I started off getting abuse – I'm one of these beaten, abused dogs who likes it now. 'Yeah, man, no budget is the way to go!'

SIMON PEGG

CG or not CG? That is the question...
Or, CG is like synthesizers

SPegg: It was extraordinary to go down to Pinewood Studios and see *Star Wars* being made, and to see it being made with so much care and attention. It was extraordinary and I feel like it couldn't be in better hands.

It was very exciting when the trailer came out because I'd seen a bit of it being made and you could see people's reaction to BB8, the rolling droid. He's going to blow people away, he really is. And to see all the practical effects...

What I feel like, is with CG, it is a little like synthesizers. When synthesizers happened, everybody was like, 'This is it, guitars are dead, drums are dead, it's all going to be synths,' and then eventually it found its way into the pantheon of musical instruments and it became part of the process. It wasn't the be all and end all of everything. With CG it was the same thing: 'Let's just use CG all the time. Nothing; you don't need masks or models any more.' And that period now has come to an end. And all the while the physical effects industry has been slowly improving and reinventing itself and coming up with new techniques.

So this film will showcase a whole new era of prop-making and reality that's going to suddenly feel so keen and vital.

The thing that CG has a problem with is presence. I say that having done a movie with a CG character, which I loved. What Double Negative did with *Paul* was create an incredible, very physical presence. They'd animate stuff around him, socks on the floor, things you wouldn't think of with CG.

SP: *So to bring it all into the room a bit more.*

SPegg: Yeah, it was very clever. And I'm not, 'Oh CG...' bemoaning it – it's an extraordinary tool.

SP: *I think with all of these developments they need to have their moment of explosion, then to be used artistically and well. I argue with people all the time who say, 'Oh, I hate 3D.' It's ridiculous to hate a whole thing. When 3D is used well— Dredd used 3D beautifully. It's another amazing tool. It's the same with CG – where it's used well and used correctly it will continue to be a beautiful addition. It's great people are realising not everything has to be CG.*

MICHAEL SMILEY

The compliments of strangers

Or, making the quantum leap

SP: *So when did comedy come into your mindset then?*

MS: That didn't really come into my head to be honest. I just lived every day as it came. I didn't realize that my interests and skills were something that could create employment. It was a quantum leap from being a massive Billy Connolly and Robin Williams fan, knowing *Live at the Met* backwards or Billy Connolly backwards or quoting *Life of Brian*, cracking jokes and being the funny guy in the bar. I didn't see that as, 'Well why don't you do that then?'

Somebody said the first time they heard Elvis Presley they went and formed a band; I never made that quantum leap in my head. I never thought I could do the things I wanted to do, or what my heroes did. I thought that they were in another dimension somewhere and it wasn't somewhere I could reach.

SP: *It's strange where the boundaries are imposed. A lot of people wouldn't have thought to move to another country at a young age, without security or anything else, but you had the openness for that yet things like optimizing or using your natural personality traits – I guess in a way it's too obvious. It's just you.*

MS: I've thought about this long and hard. I didn't have anybody in my life growing up who thought, 'Do you know what, you're really good at that thing, why don't you do that thing?' So there was no Yoda character in my life. My dad and ma had their interests, so did my sister and brother. You had things you did when you weren't working. You got your job and that helped you when you had your free time: you'd done the things you like and then you'd done your job.

SP: *I mention this all the time: growing up in Essex, it was years before I even considered what working in London meant. That was everyone's goal – to go and work in the city. No one told me what the job we were all trying to get was, it was just working.*

MS: *Boys from the Blackstuff* was on around that time – it was 'Give us a job'. You know what I mean? Coming to London as well, and this is the way your life starts to come together despite yourself sometimes. I was saying earlier on, when I came to London I was exotic to some extent, to certain people I became friends with, and then they'd seen qualities in me that they then highlighted. So I had friends constantly going, 'Well why don't you go and do that? You should do that.'

I was a bicycle courier and there was a courier magazine called *Moving Target* and I used to send little snidey silly letters – anonymous letters – and then got this guy Buffalo Bill, he was the editor, to allow me to write for them. I showed them to a friend who was working in the BBC, Kim, and she said, 'That's funny, you should be writing for radio. There's this thing called *Weekender* and they always look for uncommissioned writers.' Their commissioned writers were people like Stewart Lee and Al Murray, and Armando Iannucci and Harry Thompson were the producers. So I wrote a couple of bits and got some bits in, which then made me go, 'Oh, maybe I can do this…' The penny dropped with me.

SP: *Again, it's that simple thing of someone going, 'Yeah, this is good. Good to the extent that we're using it.'*

MS: The confirmation of people who don't have to give you a compliment is the big one. Your ma always told you you'd be great and you're the smartest boy and the most beautiful lad in the world, and your dad said, 'Well done our lad.' But if a complete stranger who would rather walk past you turns around and goes, 'That was good, here's some money for that bit of good you just done,' you listen.

MICHAEL SMILEY, cont'd

Don't mug yourself off

Or, we can always do better

SP: *How was your transition into TV and film acting? At what point did you feel you became an actor?*

MS: Because I'd never acted before, what I wanted to do was to try and be somebody. For me the feeling as an actor when I thought, 'Ah I'm proud of that, that was OK,' was quite recently actually, when I started working with Ben Wheatley. In other jobs it was just saying other people's words – you were shape-shifting and just being whatever the character was.

When I played Pringle in *Down Terrace* the character was written for me. I was allowed to improvise. So as soon as I got there, I realized I was in safe hands and it was going to be fun. I relaxed. And that's half the battle. Be prepared but also be relaxed as well. Relax into it. Be confident you're going to give a good performance.

Up until that point I didn't want to let anybody down, I wanted to hit all the marks and wanted to learn all my lines. It was all that plate spinning, patting your head, rubbing your tummy thing that acting is sometimes. It's like when you're learning to drive and the guy says, 'Look in that mirror and that mirror and put the clutch in and change it into first and make your hands at ten to two – and you go, 'I've got to remember all that shit?' So acting was like that for me at the start. Constantly going 'Fucking hell!' I didn't want anyone to go, 'I'm sorry Michael, we've really persevered with you as an actor but you're going to have to leave.'

SP: *I remember reading one bit of advice recently: when you're at a casting or if you're called in for a specific thing, just remember in most of these situations it's because they* want *you to do that. It's not that they're waiting for you to fail. The ideal situation for them is that they put you in it, so be aware of that and have that mindset and be more relaxed in that. Rather than that nervous, 'I need to do everything I can.'*

MS: There's two bits of advice I was given. One was: when you're doing stand-up, when you go onstage, pretend it's your encore. So everyone's going, 'He's a bit confident!' You're going, 'Heeyyyyy, thanks for having me back!' And when you're going for an audition pretend it's your call-back. So you walk in and go, 'Hiya,' like we're already mates. And they're going, 'Who's this guy? He's alright.' And that gets you over that initial dry mouth thing. Auditions can be life sapping. I've done some horrendous auditions where I've just lost sleep about it afterwards because of that natural not-wanting-to-let-yourself-down thing. I don't want to let myself down – I'm a working-class lad who comes from a housing estate. You don't want to be mugged off; you don't want to mug yourself off.

SP: *I completely understand: I had some filming a few weeks back and I didn't sleep afterwards because I felt I could have done better. It's one* *of the first things I'm doing, so I'm not an important cog in that work, so it's something that's moved on from quite quickly – I'm not in a place to say, 'Let's have a few more takes of that, I think I can do better'. But again, I ended up being able to sleep by going, 'Someone's wrapped on it, they've got what they wanted'. I can't beat myself up thinking, I could have done better, I think I could have improved on that.*

MS: We can always do better. If you don't do it well enough they'll tell you.

SP: *It's a director's job to think of the thing as a whole piece of work. It's your job – quite rightfully – as a human to think of your tiny little bit or your specific bit you're doing now as the be-all and end-all.*

MS: But also, don't blow it out of proportion: it is what it is. You're a part of the process and if the process turns around and goes 'let's move on' then you've hit your mark.

2

THE CREATIVE PROCESS

The creative process is truly a fascinating one. I don't think I've met a single artist, writer or performer that doesn't in some way believe they've fluked it up until now, and it's all about to start falling apart and they will be exposed.

I'm damn sure I feel like that after the completion or success of anything I've worked on. 'Right. I've got away with it AGAIN. That must be it for me now though...'

And that has been the fascinating thing when discussing this topic with different guests. Often in a greedy way; whether it comes to writing or acting or performing or anything else, I have got so many tips and tools from talking to people I admire. People that I have complete faith in, continuing to produce amazing work time and time again, even if the little voice in their head echoes my own.

In many ways the creative process is something that's hugely personal and individual. But even if the advice or techniques you may hear or learn from someone else don't apply directly to you, I feel it still helps to hear them talk about them openly and honestly.

Knowing that everyone has the same doubts that you have at some point. Knowing that when your favourite writer sits down at their computer to start working on a new chapter or project, they have the exact same moments of doubt and concern that you have.

Over time they may have developed techniques and approaches to get over that quickly or figured out what motivation works for THEM to push through those moments – but they still feel them, just like you do.

And I find that HUGELY reassuring while I sit watching TV as my laptop, full of unfinished projects, growls at me from across the room...

AMANDA PALMER

When art and business collide

Or, respect the artist's choice

SP: *When you were touring you asked a local band to come and play at the shows and it caused quite an uproar because people were saying, 'No, musicians have a fee and a standard.' And it's something I've had problems with online before. I've done contests or campaigns with small bands on my label where I've said, 'If there are any artists who'd like to submit a design then that'd be great.' In our minds it's, 'cool, this is a cool collaboration/interaction'. But people then got furious and said, 'No, there's a fee and a price.' And neither side is wrong, really.*

AP: I think the importance in all of these exchanges, whether it's 'submit a design' or 'come play on stage', the main point that seems to get missed by the people who are criticizing it is that it's a mutual exchange. And I'm totally allowed to ask you, and you're totally allowed to say no. But if both people step up and say, 'Yes, this is mutually beneficial: I want to invite you, and you want to come to my gig', then the outside judgement really doesn't understand the system.

SP: *I couldn't agree more. I'm fine with someone responding and saying, 'My art has a value, and you're asking me to do it under that, so I'm not willing to do it.' That's fine. It's when they're imposing it on other people who were maybe excited or enthusiastic to be involved in a project. Then it seems unfair.*

AP: I fell into this deeply when I was dealing with this particular controversy. Specifically, I asked string players and horn players of basically any talent level – they had to be above a grade school level but they didn't have to be great, they just had to be able to read charts – to come and play onstage with my band so we could beef up some of the songs. And we didn't really have the budget to tour and get an extra tour bus.

This is the important thing to understand: if no one had said yes, we probably just wouldn't have done it. And that is important to understand. I tried to get a handle on, why now? Why is this so upsetting to people *now*? And I think, on the one hand I had made a lot of money – or *seemingly* made a lot of money out of Kickstarter. No one knew what my actual nets and grosses were, they just saw the giant blinking sign in the sky. But also, if you look at what's happening in general with the crumbling infrastructure of how artists are getting paid, it's no wonder journalists are freaking out now, specifically, about people asking them to work for free, and that musicians are specifically freaking out *now*. Because if you're a classically trained violinist, your work opportunities in 2015 versus 10 years ago or versus 20 years ago are just dwindling ever further downward, and so you're getting testier and more frightened. And for those looking for something to blame it's easy to look at me and go, 'It's people like Amanda Palmer.' But that's actually bullshit. I'm not the culprit at all.

Garbage just went through this because they asked if any photographers wanted to submit photos they'd taken for a book. And they got the exact same thing: one of the photographers wrote this scathing open letter saying, 'You are Garbage, how *dare* you ask me to submit my work for free when you're this giant band and I'm this photographer.' And of course you know whose side I'm going to land on. They can ask, you can say no. Just say no! It's fine! Or tell them, 'You know what, my work is really great. Can you at least give me five hundred bucks? And I will give you these ten images because I'd really love to be involved in your project, but I really do need the money.' And then they can say no, and that's fine.

It depends on the project, ultimately: you don't want to walk into a music studio and work with an engineer who's just psyched to be there. I'd be more excited to work with the guy who says, 'Here's my day rate, I'm an engineer, this is my studio day rate, this is what it costs.' It's all context. That's different from making a video on a rooftop with a budget of a thousand bucks, where it's going to expand and contract depending on how many people decide they want to show up and paint themselves naked.

There's a movement against unpaid interning for sort of the same reasons. I've been an unpaid intern – I interned in a record store. Just to be around. The thing I keep pointing out to all these people who criticize – the photographer with the angry open letter – my band played two years of gigs pretty much for free. We played my house, my friends' houses, any art gallery opening... Basically anyone who asked us if we would gig, we would gig. I sort of look back to those times, and if we had initially refused to play without payment, my band would have gone fucking nowhere. If we'd said, 'But we're musicians, and our work has value and you have to at least pay us $100,' we would have just been passed over. Because the people didn't have the budget or it wasn't worth it to pay the band. But it was worth it for us to play the gig. So in all of these situations it just comes down to: respect the fucking artist. Respect the artist's choice to do it or not.

ALAN MOORE

Comics and class

Or, Mickey Mouse was an anarchist

SP: *Comic books, especially back in the sixties and seventies, were the only place you could really have no limitations. You could do anything. The only limitation was your imagination; it could take you absolutely anywhere.*

AM: Yes, and there's a class element in that. Comic strips on both sides of the Atlantic were originally designed for the working classes, who were considered to be illiterate and unable to read without the aid of pictures. That was the audience, and so that's what nearly all of the comic strips focus upon. It was all class-based humour. Over here the first comic strip was *Ally Sloper's Half Holiday*, which was about a Victorian drunk and his lowlife family and friends. Over in America it was *The Yellow Kid*, by Richard Outcault, which was in one of the

Hearst newspapers, and was considered to be – because it was printed in colour with the kid wearing a bright yellow nightshirt, yellow being a colour that everybody associates with well-being and happiness – a cheap trick by Hearst to get readers to buy his paper, even though the content was heading for the gutter.

SP: *It was seen as uplifting.*

AM: Yes. And that's where we get the phrase 'yellow journalism'. But it was all about a kid who lived in the slums. In *Blondie*, Blondie was originally a lower-class flapper and Dagwood [her husband] was a member of the aristocracy whose parents frowned upon the marriage. So it all started out like that. Then, when America tended to merge towards the middle class, you see all of the originally anarchic and lower-class characters become suburbanized. Mickey Mouse starts out as a spiky anarchist who does horrible cruel things to animals; give it ten years, he's living in the suburbs, he's wearing a short-sleeved shirt, he's got a couple of nephews... Dagwood and Blondie are now in a middle-class suburban American neighbourhood.

SP: *It's crazy; the underlying yet completely natural mirroring of society through stuff that many would see – particularly at that point – as quite throwaway. Comics can now be used to document the changes in society and everything else.*

AM: That is perhaps, at the end of the day, the best use for pop culture. Yes, there is the thrill of it at the time. There is what we all enjoy about it when we first hear that single, or first read that comic, or first read that book. There is that thrill. But, years later, decades later, the real value of the thing is very often in how it reflected its times and what it said about its times.

For example, with the comics that we were talking about, it's worth noticing that superhero comics, when they first came into being, that was two working-class boys from Cleveland and *Superman* was a vision of working-class empowerment. He was brought up in a rural environment. He was the first and last superhero to come from such an environment. All of the ones that came after him were wealthy playboys, doctors, were arms manufacturers: these were all very solidly ensconced in the middle class. That's the big difference, the shift between the origins of the character and the kind of industry that came out of it. But it's right what you say: our trash culture is often our best indicator.

SP: *It can often come across as the least thought about, and therefore the most subconscious, of the lot. It's not overly analyzed and broken down, like, we're doing this article and we need to be careful of what truths we're telling. Trash culture is more just, here's some stuff, and you don't realize how much it's telling of the time.*

AM: What I'd say is, if you've ever worked in that trash culture, working for comics with a weekly deadline or even a monthly deadline, those constant deadlines – you don't really get the time to edit your subconscious impulses in the way that you would do in a more refined medium or art form. So you do get things kind of leaking through. You look at the Godzilla films, which, for Toho pictures, when they started out, these were trashy, quickly made films.

In the first Godzilla films, it's very difficult to escape the idea that this is in some way Japan's response to having atom bombs dropped on Hiroshima and Nagasaki; that this is a big atomic monster that flattens cities. However, you move on a bit and Japan's relationship with nuclear power is becoming a bit more nuanced, and, yeah, Japan was relying on nuclear power. So suddenly nuclear power was our friend. And consequently, in the later Godzilla pictures, Godzilla was our friend. He's living out on Monster Island with Mothra and all the other nice monsters, and they only intervene when some alien monster turns up and threatens to bring down the property values or whatever. So these are pro-social monsters by the end of it. As is nuclear power: a pro-social monster.

SP: *It is crazy how, when we look at it with the benefit of hindsight, the times were reflected so clearly and obviously in those things.*

ALAN MOORE, cont'd

Taking responsibility for your life

Or, the first magical decision

SP: *So you started off as the artist, as the writer, as everything. How was it to go from that into an industry where you've suddenly got deadlines, and you have to choose which part to hand over?*

AM: This was a learning process for me. I originally came out of The Arts Lab scene, where the idea was there was no reason everybody can't do a bit of anything. You could try all sorts of things and you would find that, actually, involving yourself in a lot of different disciplines, there's a cross-fertilization process. Like when I did stand-up poetry. I'd been writing it and publishing it in my little poetry fanzine that I was producing when I was at school, but when I actually stood up and had to read it, I suddenly realized that because a thing looks good on the page, that doesn't mean that it's going to work as a piece of performance. And that's when I started to realize the importance of rhythm, and this eventually fed back into all my other writing because I realized that, if I'm writing a piece of prose, even though the reader can't actually hear me reading it, the reader has got their own voice in their head and that's following a rhythm too.

SP: *It's being performed in some way.*

AM: Exactly. So all of these things, they help each other. They help you in all of the different fields that you're working in. Now, when I first decided that I wanted to make a living out of doing something I enjoyed – and it was originally as broad a notion as that...

SP: *It's not to be underestimated how big a decision and notion that is.*

AM: Oh, it's gigantic.

SP: *Growing up, where I lived, we were just near London. And at school the goal of everyone was to get your grades, go and work in London, and earn money. It was only years later that I realized that I didn't know what working in London was. It wasn't specific to a job. You go into the city, you earn money, you come back. There wasn't a notion of 'I need to do something I'm passionate about or I enjoy'. So it's an easy one to throw in there, but it's a huge choice to say, 'That's how I want to make my living'.*

AM: Well, retrospectively, I can see that that was actually the first magical decision that I made in my life, which was simply that nobody else was responsible for my life other than me: that there was nobody trying to hold me back, there was nobody trying to help me forward. That it all came down to me and once I'd taken responsibility for everything, I found that everything started to work just fine. And that was a huge and empowering decision.

SP: *It's hard for people to realize how much you own both success and failure when you're in complete control. A failure that's your own, I can accept that. A failure where I feel I can blame someone else or I feel someone's let me down or held me back, I'll stay awake at night thinking about that for hours.*

AM: My failures: I'm completely big enough to carry them. That's not a problem. It's only when you get something that is compromised, that is not your fault, where you've done all the work that you could possibly be expected to do and it has still broken down. That's much more difficult to take. So when I started out, that was my only agenda.

KURT SUTTER

There's no such thing as a bad draft

Or, it's the discipline of doing

KS: Still to this day the desert is one of the places that settles me. I love it. I came to LA and did what you do: tended bar, auditioned… My sense of timing with acting has always been bad though. I literally landed in LA during the tail of the first writers' strike. Fucking nothing going on. I found a good group of friends and was there for a while, but it was in LA that I was becoming aware, perhaps, of my substance abuse issues and tried to clean up on my own a little bit.

SP: *It's a place that tends to bring it out of people – if it's there, that's where it'll come up. It's somewhere that will send you one route or the other. Either you'll go down and it'll be bad or you'll have that support and that prompt to go, 'Right, I need to deal with this.'*

I think addiction is a word that gets used a lot and is a scary thing, but I think it depends what you're addicted to: addictions to substances are terrible; addictions to art, to studying though? I think a lot of the people who've achieved great things, whether it be in business or film or whatever area, are addicted to what they do. And that's a key to it. It doesn't have to be this dirty word.

KS: You have to be an obsessive and I definitely have an obsessive all-or-nothing personality. It's just choosing the right all or nothing. Sometimes I make the right choices and sometimes I don't.

Part of it is just sobriety and learning to trust. But the greatest thing about me being a writer is that it is so antithetical to who I am as a human being. The idea of doing a draft of something was just inconceivable to me. My approach to anything I did was: 'You're either going to fucking love it and if you don't it's a piece of shit and I'm never going to write again.'

SP: *You made a terrible choice of career there because that's what it's all about!*

KS: It's what it's all about, right? The first script I wrote after my marriage ended was good, but then I wrote five or six screenplays that were garbage. But I know that, had I not written that script first, I wouldn't have had the sense that I could do this.

I see it in my son: he'll write a song and he'll put it right up on SoundCloud and if it doesn't get the respect he wants, he'll feel, 'Oh it's crap.' All I can do is convey to him that there is no bad draft. There is no bad song. And I use fucking Springsteen as my model for that. Springsteen just has huge binders and notebooks of lyrics and of songs he never recorded and maybe never even showed anyone. When I write a script that's awful, there's always something in that script that can be used – whether a character, a piece of dialogue...

SP: *The exercise of writing and completing something is huge. Even if you spend a week writing and all of it is garbage, that's fine. You've been writing, you've been engaging in that practice. You know what doesn't work, essentially.*

KS: It's the discipline of doing it; it's the things you learn from doing it.

DANNY WALLACE

Getting the words down on paper

Or, distraction is part of the process

DW: Sometimes people ask me about writing, or about how to get an idea away, and really the secret is that the only way to do something is to do it. People think that writing a book is a completely closed shop or exclusive club in some way, but for all the people who've ever written a book there was a time when they had never written a book, and they had to write a book for that book to exist. So it's just all about taking the first step and doing something.

You have to look for moments and look for a turn of phrase that someone has thrown your way, or just a strange moment, or just anything, but you can write about anything because it's all just about life.

SP: *Having a regular weekly column to write for must be great training and exercise for writing books and everything else, because I think people forget the brain is a muscle the same as any other part of your body, so you need to exercise it. I've never been a believer in writer's block and I've had arguments about this.*

DW: Yeah, me too.

SP: *And I'm not saying you can always create amazing stuff, but you always have the ability to sit down and write something. I mean, I've had writer's block before, even though I don't believe in it, and the reality has been that I wanted to play my Xbox more than I wanted to write. I can't think of anything so I'm going to play computer games.*

DW: That's part of it: part of the process is distraction. I've told this to my wife many times, and she finally believes me, that if she walks in and I am playing Xbox or PlayStation, whatever, then that is actually part of the process. Because you might hit a slight wall or you might run out of energy, or you don't know where to go and are just doing something else for a bit. And that means that when you come back you'll have new ideas, a new angle, you won't be lost in the mire of whatever little thing was tripping you up; it won't be a problem any more.

SP: *I've always found the best way to complete something is to have another job on the go that you want to do less.*

DW: Well, when I first wrote a novel I wasn't sure I could write a novel. In part I wrote a novel to see if I could write a novel. And that was a very different process for me because in the past I'd have had an adventure; or I'd have been to some places and met some people and I would know what the story was, because I would have lived it. But now I had to deliver it in quite an entertaining way.

SP: *And there's not a great deal of looseness on what the story is with non-fiction, whereas I've had friends who've handed in what they thought were final drafts of novels who have then been told, 'I think we need to change this, this and this.' If it's a real-life occurrence, that's not such an issue, because it's like, well, no, we can't because that didn't happen; whereas if it's a novel you've got that insecurity that someone might come round and say, 'That's not how it should go.'*

DW: It can become like a puzzle you know how you put together. With novels I want the opening to be strong enough that it will spawn new ideas that will get me to the end. I'll have an ending in mind, which might change, but I'll have a beginning and an end, and then it's about the middle. And you know, it turns out they're quite important, the middle bits, but that's where you explore your characters and have your fun.

But I've come up with a technique that can help with writing, which is that you work out how many words you want to write that day – let's just say two thousand. Then you draw four boxes on a piece of paper and each of those boxes is worth five hundred words of the two thousand. And that just means that now you've got an actual target for the day, and it means that when you've done five hundred words you can tick that box, and then when you've done one thousand you can tick the next box. Then you can have a break or whatever, and what you normally find, or what I've found, is that something in that process frees something up in your mind. I think it's because you're not as concerned with what you're writing about, it's more just getting on with writing. And then you'll find that you've exceeded your target for the day. It's something that just seems to work for some people. You're changing the focus of your day.

BILLY BRAGG

The reality of living your dream

Or, when the gods want to make you mad, they first make your dreams come true

SP: *Doing the thing you love for a living is tough, because you risk ruining something, your love for something, your passion.*

BB: I mean, on the one hand you have to remember how privileged you are to be able to do the thing you always wanted to do and get paid for it. Most people don't have that privilege. But having found that life, you then have to have the courage to live it, and to not be cowed by the fact that you've got to get on the plane and go to Australia – I say that because I'm not a great flyer. I wouldn't say I'm nervous, I'm just never relaxed up there. I can't sleep on aeroplanes; I don't like it. Sometimes if it's a grey old day and the sky looks a bit mean I get on the plane and I sit there and think, I wish I was somewhere else. And then if it really gets bad I think to myself, you're flying to Australia to do a TV programme about, you know, the Chartists: imagine how long the queue of people would be to sit here and do this job now. If I turned round and said, 'Do you know what guys? I've had enough.' How long would the queue be to do this job? I'm just thinking of the people I know, never mind the people I don't know, and that kind of helps keep it in perspective, you know.

SP: *I remember the guilt I felt when we did our one really big American tour, which could be gruelling: it was 24 shows in 25 days with a TV show in the middle. I remember the guilt I felt on long drives as I was sitting there genuinely fantasizing about being back working the tills at HMV. And I felt so bad, because I was doing what everyone still working there, all my mates, would give anything to be doing. Yet in that moment, I was pining for it, and that kind of felt ridiculous.*

BB: I'm fortunate in that all the things I ever wanted to happen to me, happened to me. And it made me really happy. I know people doing this job that all the things they hoped would happen to them and more happened, and it didn't make them any happier than they were before, and that, to me, is such a terrible, terrible thing. You know, I've sat on tour buses and watched, you know, lead singers of bands just be miserable... And where do they have to go then? Where do they have to go? They've realized their dream and they feel it's made their life shit. There's not a lot you can say to someone in that situation.

SP: *There's not more you can ask for; you've got everything you wanted and you're unhappy... It's a dark situation.*

BB: When the gods want to make you mad, they first make your dreams come true, you know? So I feel fortunate in that I still love the gig I'm doing and there are still people out there interested. You know, I can go to Australia and there are people interested in what I've got to say. That's the thing that I think I'm most willing to celebrate, because it was 30 years since *Life's a Riot with Spy vs Spy.* Thirty shmirty really, but the fact that after all this time there's still people interested enough to listen to me – that's a thing worth celebrating.

TALL DARK FRIEND

The creative brain

Or, waiting for the quantum leap home

SP: *The illness you had – synaesthesia – there's a level of visualization with that, isn't there? I remember talking to someone about synaesthesia and they could see smells, or smells had a colour. Just to clarify, it's so annoying when people hear the tiniest thing and think it applies to everyone. Everything is on a spectrum, and there's a variation.*

TDF: That's so important you say that – that part, specifically. This is something I've wanted to say, it's an amazing thing about the human brain. It's a process called 'cross modal abstraction' and it's what creative people do every single day. Everyone does it every day. When we were talking earlier, I said, 'I'm going to talk about science, but don't worry, I'm going to keep it light.' And then you said, 'You can go as dark or heavy as you want.' Now, because the word 'light' is an homonym – it means light as in weight or light as in light – the opposite of that is dark or heavy. Those are ideas, variables on a paradigm, which you've taken and applied to the idea of a conversation. That's cross modal abstraction. So the darker stuff, maybe the more taboo stuff, goes in the dark section; puffy, airy, fun stuff goes in the light section. That's what synaesthesia is across the senses. You hear smell... It's not a different thing.

I don't know what you're like with people quoting your own work back to you; it resonated with me so much, I was getting a bit teary earlier when I wanted to tell you about this. One tool you have as an artist is the ability to reference pop culture stuff, because there's so much emotional investment in that, that you tap into it like a seam, and you can utilize that emotion. In 'Introdiction' on the *Distraction Pieces* album, you reference *Quantum Leap*; there's this great line about hoping that 'this leap will be the leap home'. And as a creative person, you're making all these small connections between things all the time. Like I said, this is cross modal abstraction. You don't get a choice other than to live in a life where you're being pulled in all these directions by these connections all the time. And it's great because it means you get to see all these different images other people don't get to see. But there is that sense of 'I just wish I could go home' – I'm just getting really emotional, filled up with oestrogen – just to be able to go home just for a minute. You know?

SP: *I completely relate and understand. I think so many creatives I know have a shared dream. And it's going to sound really dark and ridiculous, but I've regularly been driving home or something and thought, 'I'd love to just have a crash.' Just to have that time of resetting. I'm in a hospital bed, I can't do anything else, I just get to go into myself and be me for a minute and not be trying to do... When – as you, with books and with albums – there's so much you need to do, and so much you're pulled towards –*

you're working with schools – that it's hard to stop for a moment and go, 'I just want to leap a second.'

TDF: Even in your own mind, the connections that you make, you have to live in a different sphere to make certain semantic connections between words. Especially with spoken word, it's a good example. But then to quote another science-fiction, iconic reference, *Hitchhiker's Guide;* they've got the improbability drive and it's almost like, once you've started, once you've pressed the button, you can't turn back. You have to keep pushing it and pushing it until you've statistically returned home. So as a metaphor, it's like saying you have to keep creating and innovating until you've covered so much that you can see where home is. Or at least arrive somewhere near back to home.

SP: *It's bizarre. I was sitting in the car park before coming in and I was talking to a friend of mine, Polarbear, who's a great spoken word artist. We try and meet up every now and then, and he asked how I was doing. I said, 'I'm good, but, as you know, with me, always doing a million things, always rushed off my feet.' He said he's convinced I'm going to get to 40, shave off my beard and just look back at everything. He knows that every time we meet up I'm trying to juggle a million things. He said, 'I know there's going to be a point where you just go, "Right, cool. Let's draw a line under that for now". Even if it's just for a limited time.'*

TDF: Like with Jim Morrison, but with an opposite ethos on the beard. He kind of stopped and grew a beard.

SP: *Exactly. I was obsessed with Jim Morrison in my teens. It's bizarre that Jim Morrison was going mental for so long and the time he actually died was the point where he was off drugs, having that point where he was like, 'I'm going to take some time off, grow a beard, get fat and look at everything I've done.' And that's the time he broke.*

TDF: Almost like the body saying, 'You don't need to innovate any more, you're done.' That's this whole thing, ending to achieve a state of discordance, to reach the unknown or whatever. A state of sensory discordance. His brain's gone, 'Alright, you don't need to do any more. You're done now.'

KATE TEMPEST

When the spoken becomes the written word

Or, it's a whole different world

KT: As I've grown older, the poetry establishment has, in some ways, opened its arms; some people are still really snobbish about it and think I don't really belong there. To be working with someone like Don Paterson, who's my editor at Picador, is a big deal, because for ages – for years – I had to put my own poetry books out, to start my own publishing company, to print my own stuff. The books were always really expensive because I wanted them to look really beautiful so we had to spend loads of money. Then Picador came along, and it's a big deal: they publish poetry and it's a whole different world of poetry to the world we know. And to go into that world – I was intimidated and everything else. But I started speaking to Don and he started teaching me about what a page can do that a stage can't. He'd go, 'You can't perform a semi-colon but on the page it's doing a lot,' and like all this kind of stuff.

I get a real buzz out of the fact that I'm now a published poet. And that my collection exists and it's published by the same people that publish, you know, Carol Ann Duffy or Glyn Maxwell or Robin Robertson, all these people I didn't really know about before, but now I'm reading. I'm reading poetry on the page and I'm thinking about myself as a writer and all this kind of stuff. I'm still a rapper at heart, I'm still a musician. I've been desperate to make music forever and for a long time I was making music and it wasn't going very well. So the fact that now the music's out and I'm doing that and I'm pursuing that side of my creativity but at the same time I'm growing, trying to write a novel, trying to be a writer, trying to be a writer of different kinds of things, it's like...

SP: *It's all writing, right? It's all writing.*

KT: It's writing, but it's just, it's mental – I can't even quite explain myself properly because it's such a weird mixture of feelings. Like, I still feel like I'm trying to prove myself all the time, and even as you do more, the more you do the more you've got left to prove, it's weird.

SP: *I think it's good. I often end up bringing things back to mixed martial arts, but there's a thing in Brazilian jiu-jitsu where it's never good to be the best person on the mat: it's always good to have someone better than you; you should always be a white belt compared to someone.*

KT: Yeah, yeah, yeah.

SP: *So that's the thing if you're drifting in between worlds. It's like, right, I'm killing it here, and then I continue to kill it here, but if I'm going to do that I need to have something that I'm the white belt at, I'm the novice at; that I'm learning, to keep myself hungry rather than just go, I make albums, I kill it. It's always having that thing, always be a white belt at something. I think that's key.*

It's fascinating you were saying about the page of poetry because that's something I've never really written, or never really read or known much. But it was something a few years ago that my brother really politely said to me, obviously knowing I'm a spoken word artist, he's more into page poetry because of the greater width of the parameters, or the less constraints and the more that you can do and the things, as you were saying then, the things that you can do on page that you can't do onstage. Onstage there's a lot you can do but it's still kind of restricted and it's something I never thought about. I like doing it onstage because I perform it how it's meant to be, rather than someone else having their own interpretation or reading it in a certain way, I put it across how it's meant to be heard.

So how exciting has that been, finding your voice on page. Because I think it can become a crutch if you're a good performer, which you are, obviously. If you're a good performer it can become a crutch, because you can make a decent poem sound amazing by your performance of it, whereas on paper you've not got any back up there: it is what it is.

KT: Yeah, definitely. You can get away with a sloppy line, you can get away with clichéd rhymes. You can do a lot just from repeating something that suddenly makes it sound more powerful than it did the first time, you know. And when I was working on stuff to be put in this collection, this book, I sat down with the editor, I delivered the draft, and it came back and he'd underlined all these things I'd never thought about the content.

I know it's a funny thing for a poet to say, but when you're writing really instinctively and you write it and you perform it, suddenly that's the poem, because you said it out loud and it worked: that's the poem now. But when you write it down for the page, you're looking at it and it's like, 'Why is that word there?' 'That's like a really baggy kind of analogy, you don't need that.' 'Really, is that where you want to finish this? It should finish six lines earlier.' All this really rigorous headspace where suddenly I realize that I could just be clearer, more cohesive; it could be better. And I'm still such a novice with it, but for me it's exciting. Exactly as you're saying, like mixed martial arts – there's always so far to go, and spoken word as a scene is pretty small and you can kind of get away with feeling like you're smashing it, but actually there's so much more that I want to do with my writing.

SP: *And that's it: when you've got your fan base, you can't go back to that day when you didn't have a fan base. So when you've got your fan base there's a lot that they will allow you to get away with because of their love of your work in general, and I think that's a dangerous thing.*

KT: Yeah, and then you become like a caricature of yourself almost. Then you're doing Kate Tempest, rather than turning up and you've got this new thing and you want to kind of try something out. But it's the same with writing for theatre. I had no idea how to do it, I'm still learning. Same with the novel, same with music. It's like everything I'm trying to write now I want to be better than it was yesterday, I want the next thing to be better. And it feels good that, it feels good.

RUFUS HOUND

Art vs Commerce

Or, you'll never get luckier than fatal
pancreatic cancer

SP: *Recently I had someone suggesting I was taking sponsorships on my Instagram feeds. They said they'd noticed that a lot of posts recently were just advertising and they were sure I was making good money for it. I looked through, and the main one he had issue with was after Christmas and the two, three days after that, when I didn't really leave my house, and the only real good delivery near me is Domino's. And after three days of everyone being 'Christmas! Family!' on social media, I posted a picture of a few-foot-high pile of Domino's boxes.*

RH: Which is a reference to your own slovenly nature.

SP: *Yeah, it's what I've done, it's not an advertisement. But it suddenly made me think, shit, that cost me! I should have sold my soul and been paid by Domino's. Even if they'd just given me the pizzas for free, it would have balanced things out. But the reality half the time is if someone approaches you to advertise something and it's something that you regularly use, it's a really weird quandary.*

RH: The man most often quoted about the grey area between – well, not even the grey area, that's sort of the point, that it's hard black and white – between, are you an artist, or are you a salesman, is Bill Hicks. You know: if you work in advertising, kill yourself. That's how hard he is. And obviously he was much bigger over here than he ever was in America. I've now read enough biographies and books about Hicks that his friends were saying that was really much more born out of the fact that Jay Leno, who was making millions and millions of dollars a year, I'd say, at the height of his fame – although he went on to have *The Tonight*

Show so it wasn't at the height of his fame by any stretch – but as he was breaking through and he was earning all this money, he then did this huge Cheetos campaign where he was the face of Cheetos. And Hicks's fury was, you're meant to be a comic, you're meant to be one of the good guys, you don't need the money, and yet you're still telling Americans 'Hey, here's what you need! Overly salted corn-based deep-fried, you know, throw 'em down you.' And that was where that anger came from.

Hicks had psoriasis and there was an aloe vera gel that he used all the time and found it was the only thing that helped him. And he said to his mate, 'Do you know, if these people ever said to me do you want to come and advertise aloe vera gel, I'd do that, I would totally do that.' So that to me then became the line: if it's something I would use…

SP: *I used to love that as well, and I was completely drawn in by Hicks's 'you're choking on the devil's dick' line.*

RH: Satan's cock.

SP: *Satan's cock and all this. I was completely drawn in by that, and I remember when Iggy Pop first started doing insurance adverts I was furious and disgusted, but even in the time since him doing that, let alone since Hicks saying what he said, things have changed hugely.*

I think we live in a society where – I try not to discuss it online too much because I have my opinions because of the industry I'm in – people feel entitled to have a lot of stuff for free, and not pay for it. They feel it's a free system where they can have music free, have comedy free, have film for free. If that's the case, I don't think you can then impose your own moral guides on how those people earn the money that you've stopped giving to them: 'I would have loved to earn all my money from you, sir, thank you very much, but you've stopped giving me money, so now I'm earning it from these big evil people, because I need to keep doing this.'

I think it's changed hugely, but it's just such a tough subject because so many people are so opinionated on it, and, again, I don't think it's black and white. There's a lot of advertising that I obviously wouldn't do – I've never personally done any adverts and a lot of people think it's a moral thing but it's not. I just haven't thought about it enough. If something came in that was good, and it paid enough, I'd be, 'Yeah, cool.'

RH: People say, 'Stewart Lee doesn't even do corporate gigs.' You ask him, he's like, 'I would do them, I would do them, it's just that what I do does not translate to those environments at all.'

SP: *Stewart Lee used to have a bit in his set where he just says how much he hates Hicks, because he had the audacity and greed to go and die, you know. He had to do maybe three hours of good material, while the rest of us have to stay and every year come up with a new hour, a fresh hour that's still good and still on point. Hicks lucked out there; he did his three hours...*

RH: You'll never get luckier than fatal pancreatic cancer.

NICK FROST

Finding focus in the creative process

Or, I always think I'd do well in prison

NF: I went off and wrote the first draft we ever wrote of *Paul* because Simon was busy and he didn't have a chance to do it, so I went and booked myself into a nice hotel for two weeks – in London, in England. And you could rent out the living room which kind of looked out across an amazing lake and a forest and hills.

SP: *Beautiful.*

NF: And you know every morning they'd bring me two boiled eggs and a cappuccino and— It's that thing of getting a routine, and I sat there for two weeks and wrote the two hundred-page first draft of the thing, you know. I think if you're paying for it yourself there's a focus to get it done.

SP: *And routine is just ridiculously key, I think. I've said this before with touring, I'm really good at being healthy on tour, because I've got so many* *routines that are: you need to be up at this time, at the venue at this time doing this. It's easy to add stuff, so, right: I exercise at this time, I eat at this time, you know, yeah. I guess, as much as we want to be these wonderful free beings, the reality is as humans you're most productive when you're locked into a routine.*

NF: Yeah. And in small rooms. I always think I'd do well in prison. Do you know what I mean? I like that containedness. All you've got is two little shelves full of books and *Nuts* and *Zoo*.

SP: *I've always felt a prison stretch is what's stopping me from getting in really good shape.*

NF: I think that's why I liked Israel so much. It was like a prison. It was like the army, you know? You'd get three aerogrammes on a Tuesday and four hundred cigarettes on a Thursday and there'd be a disco Friday – and I liked that. That compartmental lifestyle.

SP: *Well, I think comparing Israel to prison in the current political climate is the perfect point to end on.*

GEORGINA CAMPBELL

When true life and art collide

Or, connecting with a character

GEORGINA CAMPBELL

SP: *When you got the role in* Murdered by My Boyfriend *– for anyone who's not seen it you should, but it's a story of domestic violence and spousal abuse – how much research and looking into domestic abuse did you have to do? It must be tough when it's a true story from a research point of view and building a character.*

GC: It was done by BBC Learning, so they had a massive department doing a lot of research. When it came to it, Royce [Pierreson, co-star] and I didn't see that much of the actual case research. They spoke to the family members; they spoke to other people involved in the case. Every scene in the production was real – they found people who said Ashley had told them about it herself, or they were there.

SP: *It's good if you have the faith in a writer and a team, and it's all laid out for you like that.*

GC: I think Paul [Andrew Williams, director] was smart. Obviously Royce and I did our own research, but Paul said, 'Don't get too caught up in the fact it's a real person. It's going to be really difficult not to, but you're not these people. You're doing a universal story; it is their story but if you get too bogged down in who these people are you're just going to get lost in it.' So there was a lot of research but Paul kept it so we didn't get too caught up in that. It was heavy stuff to carry with you.

I don't think he'd mind me saying it, but Paul wasn't initially sure I was right for the part. He thought maybe I wasn't sure of myself and that I wouldn't be able to step up to it. It's a tiring process, being in every scene. I remember him, in my audition, pulling me to the side and saying, 'Stop acting, just do it. Stop doing your acting face.' Cheers. Me and my acting face! But he said I proved him wrong.

SP: *As silly as 'stop doing your acting face' sounds, it's why it came across as so natural. It didn't feel like a tight witty script, it felt what it's actually like on a night out. How was it getting through the actual shoots? It's such a heavy subject. It's a dark tale. So how was that, to get through those days and those scenes? Was it hard to switch off?*

GC: It was one of the best jobs I've been on, which is bizarre considering the subject matter. But it's the best cast and crew I've worked with. Everyone was so lovely and had a great energy to them. Paul made sure nothing was ever too heavy on set – it was when you were in the scenes, but when the scenes broke he made sure we were joking around and keeping things fresh.

SP: *It's gallows humour, like in emergency rooms. There's a lot of laughing and joking because if you don't, that could crush you. You're in hugely serious situations, so if you can snap yourself out of it in some way afterwards, that's key. I was on tour when it initially aired but I remember seeing so many people talking about it online. It wasn't from the BBC Drama department so it wasn't one of the big things they pushed: it just came out and the reaction from the public was the thing that brought it to the forefront.*

GC: It was insane. The amazing thing about Twitter is you can contact people or they can contact you from all over the country and beyond. So lots of people got in touch with me about their own experiences and were saying how happy they were to see something that showed what they went through and to be able to share that with people. There are people in those situations who don't always know that they're in it, so seeing something like that on-screen is great because you can see where it ends up. And a lot of the time it does end up there. You might think it won't, but...

SP: *The beauty of the direction was the nuances along the way of the things that at the time did seem acceptable to Ashley, then when another character comments on it she goes, 'Oh, right...' After the job was done, you were suddenly getting a lot of really personal messages and stories, as you said: that must have ben rewarding but in some ways a sort of pressure.*

GC: People find it really difficult separating people from characters. When it went really big there was a really small time period where people were recognizing me – which never happens!

SP: *It felt so real that, watching it, you felt like that was someone you could see walking down the street. So when people did see you walking down the street, it must have been confusing.*

GC: Yeah. People would come up to me and talk to me about their experiences and say, 'And you've been through it too...' And I'd have to say, 'I haven't – I haven't actually been through that, but thank you for sharing with me; thanks for sharing that with me.' Which was quite a strange thing to come to terms with I suppose, because you feel a bit of a fraud when people tell you their stories. You feel awful that you can't have that connection with people that they feel that they have with you, but actually they have with the character.

But it's lovely, whenever you do something, to have people come up to you – especially when it's something so important.

3

MUSIC

When I started the *Distraction Pieces* podcast I had to choose a category for it to go under among the different classifications on the podcast sites and apps. Being known primarily as a musician, I figured that it would make the most sense to put it under music, but, the fact is, the podcast is REALLY hard to categorize.

Sometimes it's funny.

Sometimes it's political.

Sometimes it's incredibly heavy.

And, sometimes, we talk about music...

So I'd say at least once a month that category is true and accurate. Through touring for ten years I have been lucky enough to make some great friendships and connections with people across many genres and eras of music. I remember in one week playing shows with Mark Ronson, Billy Bragg and Saul Williams – all on different nights. They are three completely different artists, all of whom I have huge love and respect for, so I was very excited to get to sit down with some of these guys and discuss their approaches to their careers, the challenges they had faced as well as their triumphs across their different musical genres.

Some of my favourite moments have been when, for example with both Frank Turner and Frank Carter, you realize that you have a HUGE connection with someone over the music you were listening to from, say, 1990 to 1995. Learning that you were at many of the same gigs, listening over and over again to lots of the same albums, then years later actually meeting and being able to discuss it all.

Or, alternatively, I found I'd be having a guest on who was from outside of the music world and the podcast would turn 70 per cent into a nerd out over late nineties/early noughties rap artists.

Music can produce an instant connection with someone you've never met in your life. At a live show you can be in a room full of thousands of strangers and share the most beautiful and real moment without ever knowing the names or stories of any of the people around you.

In short: God, I love music.

ADAM BUXTON

An endless love

Or, being a Bowie fan

AB: This guy at school called William Mullins played me a tape that had some Bowie on it, and it instantly got its hooks in me. 'Life on Mars' was one of the first songs I heard, and it felt like a tune that was in my DNA somewhere and had been awoken by having it played in the real world. It just seemed like a timeless tune.

Then when I found out more about Bowie as a person, I found him bewitching and beautiful. I remember having quasi-sexual thoughts about him at a fairly early age and thinking that he just seemed lovely – a lovely man. I loved his voice, I was intrigued by both how beautiful he was but also how strange he was, then obviously when I saw *The Man Who Fell to Earth*, the genius of casting him as an alien there just further compounded my fascination with him.

SP: *Did you feel any fear of misinterpretation bringing your love of Bowie into the Adam and Joe radio show, where there was a lot of parody and a lot of impressions? Did you fear that would go down wrong or worry it would offend?*

AB: I don't think it was ever a worry because I think it was clear to anyone who listened to us for more than five minutes that we genuinely liked that guy. It was one of the things that bonded us. Joe was a fan but not as demented as I was; certainly I was the guy with the biggest Bowie problem.

But the eighties happened, and we as Bowie fans had to live through fairly consistent mediocrity from the Bowie camp. And there were many things to love and things to cherish from that era. And I would defend any artist's right to do things that are not necessarily what the fans want or expect, and just to get on with their lives. I think he still looks back at some of that work as being some very happy times for him. Collaborating with people he really liked collaborating with, but as a fan I was pretty gutted by a lot of it and just thought it was pretty awful. Particularly an album called *Never Let Me Down*. Ironically.

That was the first time I went to see him live. I went to see the *Glass Spider* tour where he had this colossal glass spider he constructed onstage. And he had all these crazy dancers and it was all post-apocalyptic but in a totally trashy way, so people would come out at the beginning going, 'We are the future! We are the scum children of the future! And you must die and we will fight you because we will stand up against you.' And all this kind of crazy, terrible, amateur dramatic theatre.

SP: *It's how they used to do gigs: theatrics, a monologue, props and giant spiders…*

AB: Exactly. With the *Glass Spider* tour he still had some amazing songs in that show and was in great voice, and he had Peter Frampton on stage as well as Carlos Alomar – artists he'd collaborated with before that I loved – the band sounded good, but there were just too many other moments where I thought, no, no, no, no, no.

At that point, as a young teen, I was scandalized. You know, you're so self-righteous at that age. How DARE you not do what I want you to do? This is not what you're good at. I've paid loads of money, you bastard. If there had been social media in those days, I'd have been straight on: '@davidbowie You let me down – I didn't think that was good what you did. You should be ashamed. I paid good money for that. How dare you?' All this entitled bullshit. It wasn't the greatest gig I'd ever been to but it was still exciting and fun, and certainly the biggest show I've ever been to – and ultimately it didn't put me off him in the slightest.

And I actually still listen to that album, because I have such affection for him that there's something I like about it.

ADAM BUXTON, cont'd

The live experience

Or, this is not how the record goes

AB: I'm one of these people who can be a little small-minded when it comes to live shows, when I'm used to the sound of an album. In fact, I feel less bad about this because I once saw an interview with John Lennon, where I think he was talking to Bob Harris about preferring it when he goes to a show and it sounds like the record. And I thought, well, if John Lennon feels the same way it makes me feel like less of a philistine.

SP: *I'm 50/50 on it.*

AB: It's a question of how many shows you've been to, really. And when you get a little bit more sophisticated, perhaps, or a bit more experienced at gig going, you look for slightly different things you can appreciate more, and you get into the musicianship and you enjoy it when they reinvent tracks or start riffing on something or, I don't know what. But when I first started going to gigs it just used to wind me up. I'd be like, 'No, no, no, this is not how the record goes!' Because I had such a strong personal relationship with these things: I'd listen to them on my Walkman, I had my earphones on and, to this day, the joy of having that connection with a piece of music is some of the happiest moments of my life, just listening to music. And so sometimes if you're really into a song and you go to see it live and you're waiting to hear it, and they launch into it and maybe it takes a few seconds before you realize it's the song that you like and it's like, 'What?!'

SP: *And you've been waiting all this time.*

AB: Yes! There were a couple of times when I saw Gorky's. They hadn't been going that long when we saw them, I don't think, and some of their stuff is so ambitious: very nicely produced, but weird sounding. It was just impossible to reproduce it onstage. And also Euros is playing away on the keyboard, he's banging his head and he's going crazy and he's also supposed to sing all this stuff, so you just couldn't get all the subtlety and nuances of what he was singing on the record. It was impossible to do it live. But it was still a great show.

SP: *There has to be a balance between what works live and accuracy. You can get away with almost anything if you're good live. If you do a different version, you don't care if it's amazing. I remember seeing Prince – there were so many different versions of things but it was just amazing because him and his whole band are just such talented people that you can't be unhappy. You'll go home and realize, 'They didn't play this, they didn't play that', but what they did do was such a spectacle they can get away with it.*

AB: Some bands do just sound so good because they're such talented musicians, and, also, they have such good support from their techs. Radiohead, I suppose, are an obvious example who spring to mind. You go to see them and they might be playing stuff you've never heard before but it's really exciting because it sounds like you're listening to it on the record. You can hear what everyone's playing, and Thom is a talented singer to the extent that everything he's trying to do is coming across, and it's just great. You're never bored. So if you're a fan and you go and see them, chances are, unless they have insurmountable technical problems, it's going to deliver.

BILLY BRAGG

Learning your stagecraft

Or, on Saturday night you're the soundtrack for
people who are trying to get shagged

SP: *The first time I met your son it gave me a very important revelation
and realization in life, if I ever choose to have a child myself. We were
chatting and you were, intentionally, I think, embarrassing him a little
bit at points, or certainly he was reacting as if Dad was embarrassing
him. It was a wonderful realization that if I decide to have a child I will
inevitably embarrass them – every child's dad will always be embarrassing, because if your dad's Billy Bragg and it's still embarrassing...*

BB: Course it is. I'm still his dad. It's just one of those things; I mean,
particularly at a gig when everyone's around, you know, fawning a bit
and everything. That's really annoying if it's your dad. So, bless him,
he's in a band now but he doesn't allow me to come to his gigs for that
reason; he likes to keep it separate.

But when we did Hammersmith Odeon last year I had three bands
on and loads of people came on and played. He sat in the wings and just
watched the stagecraft of it. He writes his own songs, but sometimes
he comes home and he says, 'You know, Dad, I lost the crowd tonight;
I don't know what I did. I did this, I did that and I did this, and it normally happens, and it didn't happen', and we sort of talk about it.

SP: *That's great to have that advice. We had Frank Turner on last week
and we were discussing how, for both of us, seeing you control and have
a crowd in the palm of your hand with just you and a guitar was a huge
lesson in stagecraft, and it's good to be able to hand that off directly.*

BB: It can be done. Some nights they get away from you, you know,
sometimes circumstances are above you. You know, a particular conversation I had with the boy: it was Saturday night he was playing, and they

were talking at the bar, and he couldn't get their attention... And I was like, Jack, on Saturday night you're providing a soundtrack for people who are trying to get shagged. Unless you're the main act and they've paid for a ticket to see you, a band like yourselves, you've just got to go at it; you've just got to overcome that and do your best show. You know, almost to spite them. Really, really lay it all down there, and I think he's got that idea; he doesn't let much throw him in that sense.

SP: *If you get the right mindset on it, it can end up being a weird motivation in those situations. I remember me and Dan early on did a show where we were on at one or two o'clock in one of the rooms in a club that had multi-rooms that were themed, and one of them was a karaoke room – they sold hot dogs in this club, it was a weird place, and we were in, like, the Aspen ski lodge. And we're playing and it wasn't a pleasant scenario to be doing your stuff, but four or five people had turned up specifically for us and we put on one of the best gigs we've ever put on, because we felt, right, they've had to sit through this shit up until now, and now they're here to see us. So rather than going, 'Oh, there's only a few people here who care,' we figured we needed to go out and put on a full show for these guys.*

BB: You owe it to whoever's there, and if the crowd is there and they're not interested in you, then you owe it to yourself to get their attention in some way or other. My apprenticeship, such as it was, as a solo performer was mostly done in a pub just south of the Blackwall Tunnel, which was called The Tunnel, and in the early eighties, in 1982 when I was first starting out solo, they had music on there – Thursday, Friday, Saturday nights – and I initially got a gig on Thursday night, for beer money, really, for nothing. Which was fine by me because I just had to get down there and it was no cost to me; I was living in Barking. And I just had to open for whoever was on. Some nights it was a heavy metal band, some nights it was a funk band, one night it was a band called True Life Confessions who had two strippers and a stand-up drummer.

I just had to take them on and one of the most annoying things about the gig was that in the far corner they had a video jukebox playing – this was at the height of the video craze – and they didn't switch it off when I was on stage. The sound was down but the video was on, so people would be watching. So I used to have to riff on whatever was going on there, stupid things happening in the video, trying to keep their attention. And eventually it just sharpened me up, you know.

SP: *It's how you grow, right? It's the tough gigs that do that.*

BB: Yeah, and because I was going every week I kind of got a handle on it, so I sort of progressed from Thursday to Friday to Saturday, and eventually I could pull a little bit of a crowd myself. So I think you need that experience, but there are always those gigs where, for some reason that you can't put you finger on, it just falls flat, or you feel it falls flat.

I don't think you can ever really be absolutely sure about audience reactions. I once did a gig where my voice disappeared completely; the whole top of my register disappeared. It was in Minneapolis. I knew it in the sound check, and I said to my manager, 'Man, I'm not going to be able to sing tonight, I've just got no voice. What's going to happen?' And he said to me, 'You know, Bill, nobody comes to hear you sing, don't worry about it, just do what you normally do.' And I went out there and it ended up I played the songs and they sang the songs.

And I felt really bad about the whole thing. Every time I go to Minneapolis someone says, 'Oh, that was such a great night, I really enjoyed it. Why don't you do one of those gigs again where we all just sang the songs?' I was just leading them through it and they were choosing the songs! It was awful for me, from where I was standing, but they enjoyed it!

BILLY BRAGG, cont'd

The communion of the live performance

Or, you can experience a download, but you can't download an experience

SP: *It's crazy that gig attendance is still as high as it is, and it feels – at the moment – like the one thing that it seems almost impossible to break in the music industry: the live experience can't be put on CD, can't be burned, can't be manufactured.*

BB: Thank God. The photographers are fucked. The filmmakers are fucked. Writers are fucked. We've still got the one thing that people can't get many other places outside of church and football, and that is communion. Being in a room with a load of like-minded people singing along at the top of your voice to a song that you love, with the person who originally sang it. Someone said to me 'you can experience a download but you can't download an experience'. You can't. That sweaty feeling in the mosh pit, you know, that anthemic moment when the person singing the song that makes you burst into tears sings it, and two thousand people sing it with you... Whatever emotion it is that this song brings up in you, that emotion is totally accepted. It could be anything: it could be the death of someone you love, it could be the unrequited love you have for someone; when everyone's singing it together and you're there, suddenly you feel like it's OK. It's OK to have this feeling. You can't get that anywhere else, man.

SP: *It's such an important shared experience. I remember I was driving home once and a Bon Jovi gig was on the radio. And, again, the radio didn't get the true feeling across, and I'm no big Bon Jovi fan, but when they played certain songs and you could hear a stadium full of people all singing their hearts out, I wanted to be there. I wanted to be there more than anything else. It's like, I'm not even into this band, but just the passion everyone has... I want to be there in that.*

BB: I mean, I never really got Oasis. It just sort of rocketed, for whatever reason, but I caught them when they played at Glastonbury. I didn't see them but I was nearby and I heard everybody singing along, and I thought, 'Oh, I see what that is now, I get it.' This is so open, these songs are so open and they're so all-encompassing that you know you're part of this.

And I think there are a lot of things now, where, because of the nature of the Internet, you don't get that feeling of solidarity. And I don't mean that in a political sense; you don't get that emotional solidarity that you're with other people who feel the same as you. Because a lot of the time I think we feel like we're the only person in the world who feels this sort of stuff, we're the only person in the world who experiences these doubts or urges or frustrations. But I think, although our situations are all different, the way we feel about them is actually quite similar, and a song can sometimes cut through all the bullshit and just put its finger on that bit in your heart, and it's released for a moment. And if that release can happen when you're at home – it can happen to you in the supermarket, something comes on in the supermarket and a song can just get you – but if you're in a crowd of thousands of people and everyone's punching the air together, it's like a breaking of an emotional wall, you know, a sort of tidal wave through a wall. And you just can't get that from sitting on your own.

AMANDA PALMER

Touring

Or, struggling with your own dickishness

AMANDA PALMER

AP: When you're on tour, you're constantly a guest in someone else's house. I think a lot of musicians struggle with this – especially when you're on the road and you're at the mercy of the environment in every situation. You're definitely constantly struggling with your own selfishness and dickishness, but you have no home, you're on the road, and you need a thing and you have to ask for it because you are actually occupied and you can't go do it, but you don't want to feel like you're enslaving the people around you. It's an art in itself. People who have been touring for years and years and have really figured out that dance are admirable to watch.

SP: *It's where people get really militant or clinical on their riders, because it's just making sure that all those small things, that aren't that important, are there so you don't have to be awkward. 'I really need some milk for my tea.' Things like that. It's an advantage; it's a skill.*

AP: It's the skill of the traveller. You've got your essential shit on you, but you're also engaged in a constant dialogue with your environment.

And you learn how to live in different environments and I've spent a lot of time doing that and I feel there's a whole sub-book of the book I just wrote [*The Art of Asking*] about how to live in other people's environments.

When I look for people to stay with, I look for their social skills much more than I look for the comfort of their actual home. Because their social skills are so much more comforting, if they're good, than having a nice comfy bed in your own room.

No one teaches you to do it, but if you're a small scrappy band staying with your friends and staying with your fans, you learn this whole sort of sub-cultural subset of how to be a guest in someone else's house every single night. And there's all these gives and takes: like, you actually do need some privacy or some space – or their Wi-Fi. But they're also hosting you and they want some social time from you, or whatever it is. You don't really talk about it as a skill, or a learned skill or an education, but it really is.

AMANDA PALMER, cont'd

A living exchange

Or, embracing mistakes in live performances

AP: I love taking little risks onstage, because it doesn't always work and sometimes you'll bring someone onstage and go, 'Just do a spontaneous thing,' and they're not good at doing spontaneous things. You just don't know. I have had plenty of moments – after ten years of almost non-stop touring – of, 'Oh shit, that didn't work.' But that's also part of the beauty of having this constant community and constant touring life, which is I'd never do the same thing twice, the audience never really knows what they're going to see. They know they're going to see something authentic and they know they might see something fail, and that's great.

SP: *I think part of the reason you have such passionate, engaging fans is exactly that. There's some excitement in the live performance again.*

It got to a point where people a few years back were going to a gig to hear a song played note for note the same as it was on a record. It takes so much out of it. I live in a small town out of London – I could stay at home and listen to the record. I've travelled for 90 minutes, I want something to go wrong. I want there to be an error, or a mistake.

AP: You at least want to feel like you're actively with the person onstage, instead of the idea that they're just up there representing something that they have to, then they're fucking off. My favourite live shows – even if the music sounds note for note like the shit on the record, maybe that's great, but there's an attitude of authenticity onstage: we are here, you are here, and we are together.

And there's so many ways of doing that, you don't have to do it in a chaotic circus Amanda Palmer way. Even with people who do high-end pop spectacle, you can feel the difference between someone who's just phoning it in and someone who means it and embraces the mistakes when they happen, instead of trying to hide them from the audience. I've gone and seen some massive pop-spectacle shows and some of them – even with their gazillion-dollar budgets – you're just bored. Because you don't feel like you're part of a living exchange.

SP: *Prince's whole band, his whole demeanour and attitude live was just... Man, they've very probably not even written down a set list. They're just that good.*

AP: Prince is in the James Brown lineage: 'I will have a band that is tight as shit.' I am in whatever the wrong lineage is. Probably the Grateful Dead lineage, where it's just, 'Hey!' I have never been very exacting about my stage players but then it's much more important to me whether I like the people I'm working with and I'm enjoying myself, even if we're as sloppy as fuck. I don't really care.

ROMESH RANGANATHAN

The Eminem debate

Or, is massive success a bad thing?

SP: *Eminem is the constant pain for me. I think he's one of the greatest of all time, but that's why it annoys me when he releases stuff that I don't dig, because he's such a natural talent.*

RR: When I first heard *The Slim Shady LP* then *The Marshall Mathers LP*, which had some more commercial stuff on it, the ideas on that record – 'Stan' was such an amazing concept for a song. Then I didn't like *The Eminem Show*, but you knew that if he wanted to, if he turned it on, he could be the best. It's so frustrating. I guess he was just off his tits; he'd do these songs where he'd just do a silly voice, and it was almost so bad that he's going, 'I hate you for liking me so I'm going to test how much you like me – listen to this.'

SP: *Did you watch* The Art of Rap? *It killed me seeing him on that because he was tighter than anyone else out there today. He's still the best technical rapper out there. But he's so hit and miss.*

RR: On Rawkus there was a compilation album – I think it was *Lyricist Lounge* – Eminem had a track on there and, man, lyrically I still think it's one of the best things he's ever done. Then you hear other things he's done and you just think, I don't understand how it's the same person.

SP: *I did a mini section on it on one of the early Beatdowns with just his battles with Everlast. Everlast would write a throwaway verse dissing him and Eminem would come back with a full three-verse track with hooks, with a break, that's as good as any song I've ever heard. And then Everlast would come back with a verse or two, and he'd be good. I'm not hating on Everlast, but Eminem would again come back with one of his* *verses, and a verse that has all of D12 on, then switch it up to mention a verse with references to Tupac and Biggie. Now you listen to some verses that are so throwaway and think, you put so much effort 'cause someone was a bit annoying!*

RR: Sometimes I wonder about comedians, when they get big – I've seen it where I've been at a gig, and you see someone like McIntyre comes out and the audience just lose it – and I always thought: it must be harder, when you're doing new stuff, to figure out what bits you're doing that are actually really good because the audience are so excited. And I wonder if that happens with someone like Eminem. He became such a phenomenon, such a megastar, that all these kids were lapping up everything he did, and maybe you just lose that edge.

ROMESH RANGANATHAN, cont'd

Hip-hop, comedy and censorship

Or, don't call me a fat bastard

RR: I've got kids now and I'm not allowed to listen to hip-hop any more. The other day I had something on in the car and the kids had got old enough to repeat stuff, and I think my wife was building up to have the talk with me. Someone had said something brutal on the record and she was like, 'No, you can't listen to this any more.' So it's a struggle.

You're giving them power by telling them they can't say things. My wife freaks out like my son's pulled out a gun as soon as he says a rude word. 'Oh my God, oh my God!' Obviously he's going to do that loads more.

It's like, there are some instances where I'd prefer someone to be racist rather than not. I was in a car accident and this guy called me a fat bastard, and I found that really upsetting that he didn't just go for a racial slur. When I first did the sketch I said, 'I'd rather he'd called me a Paki,' but the shock was too much. You say that word and they don't listen to whatever else you're saying. I censored myself because people get so distracted by that word. I remember saying it and someone saying, 'Well, you don't need to say it. It feels like you're saying it because you can, like a dick-swinging thing. "I'm going to say this, you can't stop me."' And I don't want to be that dude.

I remember getting *Eddie Murphy Raw* from the local rental place and my dad being appalled by the language. Eddie Murphy is a superstar, but he's almost unwatchable due the level of misogyny and homophobia...

SP: *The way I described it on my radio show once was, it's like watching* National Geographic *and there's boobs. It's not pornographic – we're looking at culture, we're looking at history, and that's how I kind of see it. I'm not saying this hugely homophobic and sexist stuff is acceptable, it's looking at it in a context of the time.*

RR: I wonder what would happen to my music collection if I took out any tracks that used the word bitch in a derogatory way. You'd lose so many classics.

AKALA

Holding hip-hop to a higher standard

Or, you being offended doesn't mean something shouldn't exist

A: Hip-hop is supposed to be, as Brother Ali put it, a complete plate: you've got your starters, your main course and your dessert. There should always be road rap; that's part of reality. But what we shouldn't have is every rapper pretending they've sold crack and they've shot someone: that's fake. My thing is that that should represent a small percentage because that's the reality in the endz. The vast majority of young boys growing up are working in JD Sports or going to college – and those realities are valid.

SP: *There's a US rapper on my label called B Dolan who is very political, and we've discussed how awkward it can be that the fan base you build often won't have that openness that you've just discussed there. I'll post a Lil Wayne song because I like Lil Wayne, and they'll be like...*

A: 'How dare you! Illuminati!'

SP: *Yeah – there's room for everything. I have my club night and in my club night I'm not playing much conscious hip-hop because I'm DJ'ing at 1am and I'm drunk; I don't want to hear conscious hip-hop.*

A: Unless 'It's Bigger than Hip Hop', dead prez...

SP: *Yeah, dead prez or M.O.P. or people like that... So people who are still saying shit but playing bangers. There's room for all of that.*

A: Yeah, I'm not into that. I find this judgemental attitude... I think people have got that mistake from me sometimes. Questioning the promotion of violence and misogyny in hip-hop is absolutely valid, but pretending hip-hop is different from other art forms and should be held to a higher standard than, say, Hollywood films, which do the same thing – glorify violence and misogyny and the mafia – and the FBI and the CIA; who, dare I say it, have probably done more damage in this world than young boys in the hood... Why should hip-hop be held to a different standard? It's a global conversation that affects all forms of art. And that's not me passing the buck, it's just me saying, I grew up and I love DMX and Mobb Deep and I'm not going to apologize for it now because I'm 31. Maybe I don't play that music every day, but at 15 that's what I loved. So it would be very judgemental and backward of me to act like I don't understand why 15-year-old boys and girls – particularly in difficult environments – love the equivalents. For me, DMX was creative, he was an artist; he was brilliant. It might have been very negative, but when you look at his life, what do you expect?

SP: *Exactly, and people forget that you've every right to be offended, but that isn't a reason for something not to exist: it's right to discuss and debate that but it doesn't mean it shouldn't exist. It's still a valid form.*

A: Yeah. If you take *The Merchant of Venice*: the way Shakespeare describes Jewish people in that play, in today's language, is offensive. There's no way around it. Interesting anecdote: Ira Aldridge, a famous African-American actor in the 1880s, he performed that play in Russia, but he edited the text. He refused to perform it as it was. That today would be considered a racist play. Does that mean Shakespeare was not a genius because he wrote a racist play?

FRANK TURNER

All audiences are equal

Or, we're just trying to make everyone have a good fucking time

FT: I've copped a lot of shit off various people for some of the decisions I've made about doing certain gigs, and at the end of the day, if somebody turns round and says to me, 'I don't like seeing music in venues of that kind,' that's completely legit; that's an opinion I can respect. Cool, thanks for your time before now and I'll probably see you down the line, because the likelihood is that the curve goes down again and I'll be back playing The Borderline again. If it's put like that, it's a legit comment. What is slightly frustrating is getting people saying, 'Oh, you're a fucking cunt because you're doing this, that and the other.' When actually what I've done is just continue doing what I was doing at the beginning.

SP: *I think you've got to have that view and opinion that: I'm just going to try to block out what the perception of my choice might be, and just go with what I feel I should do. If someone had said to you when you were unknown, 'Do you want to headline Wembley?' You'd be like, 'Cool, man!' If something like that's what you were dreaming of, it'd be like, 'Fucking great, all right, let's do that.'*

FT: Similarly, I've always said at the beginning that I'd open for anybody, from fucking Slayer to Steps, or whatever, because I believe that people in a crowd are equal and everybody's equally capable of enjoying what I do. I mean, I haven't put that into practice that much; I have played with some metal bands here and there, but you know if Slayer calls tomorrow...

SP: *You're down.*

FT: I'm down! Hear that, Kerry King? But yeah, you know, when I started out I always had this thing that I'll play for anyone, anywhere, any time, and that was a punk thing to say at the beginning. I continue to say the exact same thing now and people claim that that is a sell-out statement. It's like, well, hold on, make a fucking decision in life, do you know what I mean? I've never wanted to be picky about audiences because I try to treat every single person I meet as the same, as being equally valid of consideration and of talking to and of playing shows with, and all the rest of it... And that applies just as much to people going to see a big show in an arena as it does to people who make it to a squat show at the 12 Bar.

I mean, obviously it's fucking cool to be able to tell your mum you're playing Wembley, but I find it almost sociologically interesting: what's going to happen when we get that many people in a room together? How's it going to be different from playing a small show? Is it going to be different from playing a small show? Actually, to be honest – and that's the other thing as well, I mean, I feel like I'm slightly disappointing interviewers when I say this sometimes – I don't think, certainly from where I'm standing, there's much difference between a big arena show and a smaller show. Because me and my band, if it's a band show – or just me if it's a solo show – we're still doing the same shit that we would be doing if it was any venue; we're trying to engage the crowd and try to put across the art that we're making in a way that's interesting to people. And try to make everyone have a good fucking time.

FRANK TURNER, cont'd

The reality of touring

Or, I want to sit in a dark room with the curtains closed

FT: I still to this day consider that Matt from Funeral's the guy who gave me my first step on the ladder, as it were. We toured for four years then we changed guitarist after our first album and gradually fell into hating each other's guts.

SP: *Yeah, I mean, it can happen. Touring is tough. Being in a band is sort of a weird extension of the saying 'You don't choose your family but you do choose your friends' – because very often you don't choose your band; you just stumble into it. I've been lucky, I've not had that many painful tours, but you see a lot of it. You're suddenly seeing more of these people than you see of the girl you love, or your parents, or your best friend from school or whatever. They will take over that role in your life as the person you see the most. And even if they're really a decent enough person, they're not the person that you would prefer to be in that role and having to spend that amount of time with; they're someone else, therefore that's a really fucking tough set-up.*

FT: I was chatting to some guys in a young band the other day. They will remain nameless, but they were like, 'Yeah, I think we're all going to move into a house together as well.' I was like, 'Are you out of your fucking mind?!' Because they're about to start touring insanely hard, they're at that point where their career's about to break open, and it was just... Don't do that. Just give yourselves some time.

SP: *You need to be able to come back from touring and not see each other... I always have a joke at the end of every tour of saying, 'Congratulations, it's been absolutely amazing, and I don't want to hear from any of you for at least two weeks.'*

FT: Yeah, totally.

SP: *And, 'I don't want to know how you're doing – no contact please.' It's a joke but it's true as well; it's kind of what you want.*

FT: The hardest year on tour I've ever had in my life was 2013; it nearly fucking killed me, but it was great, we got loads done. We finished up in Florida and then we flew overnight back to the UK and we were at the baggage carousel in Heathrow: me, my band and crew. So there's a group of, like, eight of us who hadn't been away from each other for 12 months, and when everyone got their bags, we all just turned round and walked off; no one even said goodbye. It was just like, I've fucking had enough of you.

SP: *It's crazy, isn't it? But it's also completely natural. It's hard for people to realize that in a touring situation, particularly if you're not a massive headliner, you're sharing rooms on that tour, or sharing a bus or whatever, so in three months you've not had any time to yourself except when you're on the toilet. So there's kind of points where it's like: I want to see my girlfriend, I want to see my family, but I also want to sit and not see anyone and just watch films and chill.*

FT: Yeah, I want to sit in a dark room with the curtains closed and not talk.

SP: *Exactly. And you need that moment for it to become a happy memory again, rather than something you've just endured. When you come back everyone says, 'So, how was it? Tell me about it!' And you can feel: I've just lived that, I don't want to relive it yet, give me a week and then I'll be up for reliving it and telling you all the stories. At the moment I just want to be happy that I'm not there any more.*

FT: I'm just going through my PTSD right now.

SP: *Exactly!*

ZANE LOWE

Edutainment

Or, we found rap in a hopeless place

SP: *When I was growing up in Essex and rap was coming through it was pre-Internet, it was hard to get hold of records. How was it there [New Zealand]?*

ZL: Oh my God it was pre-import! In fact, it was pre-domestic sales! There were a couple of Street Sounds compilations that Morgan Khan put out and there was a Grandmaster Melle Mel album, and that was kind of it. Maybe a Flash album. Sugarhill Gang. I remember my friend Kirk Harding – who has stayed one of my closest friends, he manages The Neighbourhood and worked at Loud Records with Steve Rifkind for many years – we used to go and just ask him. He used to work at 256 Records behind the counter. I'd just go after school and ask, 'Is there anything new in? Is there anything new in?' I'd go every week. He'd say, 'There's a Whodini record just came in, I'll go get that.' So I'd just buy everything that came in; anything and everything that came in.

And then my mum went to New York and I said, 'Can you just bring some stuff back?' She brought back three cassettes; one was *King of Rock* by Run DMC, one was *Yo! Bum Rush the Show* by Public Enemy and one was *BAD* by LL Cool J. And I was just like, 'Oh my God, that's my summer.'

SP: *That's a hell of a trio. Good timing by your mum.*

ZL: Yeah, she was just like, 'Look I've got three cassettes.' And I was, 'I don't know which one to listen to first!' Guess which one I listened to first, bearing in mind I'm a young guy?

SP: *LL.*

ZL: Of course. The artwork! The dude's leaning against a cop car or something... I'm like, 'I'm going straight for the Hollywood blockbuster!'

SP: *Three amazing albums, but obviously LL.*

ZL: I was straight in there. First thing I hear is: 'Calling all cars, calling all cars ... No rapper can rap quite like I can.' I was like, 'What is this?!'

SP: *It's something B Dolan always goes on about. Everyone knows about tough LL and lover man LL, but people don't give enough credit to unintentionally hilarious LL. Songs like 'You Can't Dance'.*

ZL: No, no – 'Cheesy Rat Blues': it's all about this down-and-out guy who can't get anywhere. 'I take... a kiddy's tricycle'. That's one of the funniest records ever. 'Cheesy rat, you ain't all that.' It's so funny.

SP: *On one of the tours with B Dolan he had a dance battle to an LL song and one of the lines killed me: 'You dance like a fat old lady / Not saying that fat old ladies ain't nice'. It's just classic rap right there. That should be in the hall of fame.*

ZL: To me, I would really credit him and Rakim and Run from Run DMC as the three rappers who shaped my whole concept of what rap could be. And then MC Lyte. Because she had that— I hadn't heard that high-pitched voice that she brought as a female MC, a high register. But she delivered it with such fire. It wasn't, 'I'm a girl on the mic', it was, 'Hot damn ho, here we go again'. She would spit at you. And I was just like, 'Oh my lord, amazing.' But those were the crew.

SP: *I think pitch is a generally ignored thing that is essential in hip-hop. Eminem – at points he can rap so fast because he can go to that high pitch, whereas Rakim and Kane and people like that have that bass there, that authority that instantly just drives the track through.*

ZL: It's like Guru said, it's mostly the voice. I disagree with that statement a little bit, because obviously you need a lot more components, but you know what he's getting at when he wrote that line: 'I'm blessed with the larynx and I'm gonna use it.'

And when you see the great MCs and what Nas has achieved, he couldn't have delivered an album like *Illmatic* if he hadn't had a voice that was compelling enough to make you listen. If he'd rapped those in a high-energy high pitch it wouldn't have had the same impact. But when he comes out and he starts that album straight away: 'I don't know how to start this, man.' And you think, God, he sounds like someone out of a Scorsese movie.

SP: *Yeah. Him and Mos Def always sound like they could have recorded their whole album sitting down, but it doesn't make it any less immediate, or urgent and important.*

ZL: I still think the best rapping I've ever seen live in my life was the Black Star show at the Jazz Café. I watched Mos Def and Talib Kweli rapping a cappella. I'd never seen two MCs drop conscious rhymes in a way that was just so rap. I didn't feel like I was being educated, I felt like I was being entertained but in a way with words that made me think. It was just wow.

SP: *KRS-One* Edutainment.

ZL: KRS-One: 'Knowledge Reigns Supreme'. That guy – he's another one. The first time I ever heard 'Poetry'. Wow. The turning point for me was [Eric B. & Rakim's] 'Lyrics of Fury'. I heard the rhymes on 'Lyrics of Fury': 'I bless the child, the earth, the gods and bomb the rest.' Just the lyrical imagery he was coming up with. The fire. It was like he was sent from another planet, to me. I couldn't get my head around it. I still listen to a song like 'Lyrics of Fury' today and think, no one can top that.

It was just compulsive. I became obsessed with rap. And so if you become obsessed with something enough, eventually you want to immerse yourself so deep into it – whether it's football, skateboarding, or acting, or science, or whatever. For me, it was rap music.

4

SOCIAL MEDIA

Without social media you legitimately wouldn't be reading this right now. Even prior to the podcast, social media has been absolutely essential to my career. When I started out in music, Myspace was having its first boom and it was such an exciting time to be making music. The night I first started getting to grips with it happened to be the one on which a relatively unknown singer called Adele was doing the same thing. We found each other's work (through mutual friends, I think, in Dockers MC, Kate Nash and Jack Peñate) and sat up till the wee small hours messaging back and forth about different tracks we were loving on each other's page (hearing that first recording of 'Daydreamer' – that night sticks with me to this day).

After Myspace, it was Twitter for me (then Facebook and then Instagram).

The fan base and connections I was able to build through social media allowed me to have a career that, ten years on, has seen me tour the world; it's a career I couldn't have imagined having prior to the birth of social media.

Outside of my work social media has also been key. I've made dear friends, life-long connections and doomed relationships over social media, and all of them have their worth and importance in the development of my own character.

I remember being on Twitter once and seeing that Simon Pegg and Nick Frost had picked one of my songs to play on BBC Radio 6 Music when they were doing a takeover show and being SO excited! I had been a fan of those guys for years! Social media was also the digital bridge that allowed those initial, unexpected connections to develop into real-life friendships.

When it comes to the podcast, it's been even more key. Whether for booking guests or promoting episodes, social media is an essential part of the process.

But it can be a damn ugly place, too: I've had arguments on there; I've been attacked; I've had abuse; and I've witnessed people going through far worse. I've had times when social media has greatly helped my mental state, and times when it has been key in the deterioration of it.

Social Media, eh? Can't live with it, can't live without it...

AMANDA PALMER

The battering ram of Internet controversy

Or, living in a fucking bubble

AP: The connection [on social media] is a frail, fragile, untrusted and untrustable connection. If anybody from the outside world just happens to be standing at a distance witnessing your exchange and decides to yell at you, because they don't like your exchange, you are really vulnerable. I went through a year of Internet controversy and I just felt like I was getting my face punched once a week by one person or another.

The Internet makes everyone vulnerable because the exchanges are visible and they're not just those done in our village street, of 'I'll give you some bread if you walk my dog'. Usually there's no one around to judge that stuff, but all of a sudden the whole world is casting their eyes down in judgement: 'Well, we think the bread is worth a lot more than that fucking dog walking, and we're now going to attack you.'

It was sort of the growing pains of being exposed to the wider world and going, 'Holy fuck, I had no idea that you guys didn't think like me.' I didn't realize how much of a fucking bubble I lived in with my crazy, compassionate, art-fag, hippy friends. We really are different.

SP: *Everyone does the same: even though we've got this access to view the opinions of so many people in the world, of different opinions, we generally only follow people and engage with people who are like-minded. Which is completely natural, but I don't think people should be surprised* to realize not everyone thinks like them: 'Oh right, I thought the world was one way.' 'No: your world is.'

AP: The TED Talk I did wouldn't have worked and wouldn't have happened if I hadn't gone through the battering ram of Internet controversy. I felt so deeply misunderstood every time a controversy erupted of 'Amanda Palmer shouldn't be using kick-starter', Amanda Palmer shouldn't be asking her fans to volunteer', 'Amanda Palmer shouldn't be writing poems about the Boston Bomber'.

I really was shocked. I wasn't shocked at the people so far away from me who didn't get it, what shocked me was the people right next to me; the other people on the arts scene, the other musicians, the leftie journalists going, 'We don't understand how you could have compassion for someone who's a terrorist.' And going, 'Oh my God, I actually didn't know that you guys didn't think this way.'

We're all living in these filter bubbles.

JON RONSON

It's a crying shame

Or, how social media made the same
mistakes as traditional media

SP: *Social media has become such a bizarre thing. It is fascinating to highlight the fact that not only has it become acceptable to publicly shame, but often at points it's become expected or felt that you have a responsibility to shame and to publicly attack or bring people down because we all have this voice; we are all a media together, so we need to attack in this way. It's a cold and inhuman trait, and something* So You've Been Publicly Shamed *explores.*

JR: My writing *So You've Been Publicly Shamed* came out of me moving to New York. I didn't put any of this in the book, but I think it was the experience of feeling lost that made me empathize with the people being shamed: if you're feeling a bit broken, you're going to empathize with people who are being broken.

I felt like I was lost and failing in New York and I wanted to do something that reflected that. And what I started doing was stuff on 'stop-and-frisk', and hanging out with this group called The Bronx Defenders; people whose lives were being destroyed through stop-and-frisk. And just how fucked up the judicial process is.

SP: *It's fascinating in America in particular. I was watching John Oliver's show, on the bail system in America, about how crazy it is how many people are in prison because they can't afford not to be. There are certain states that have brought in a system where they can only use a bail system if the person can afford it. Which seems ludicrous but actually makes perfect sense. It shouldn't be 'If you're too poor, you should be in prison.' Which is what it's become in America. Imprisoning people on traffic charges because they can't afford not to spend time in prison.*

JR: America is the most incarcerated country in the world – the most incarceration-friendly. And yes, all these thoughts were swirling around. I was trying to figure out how to do something on justice and couldn't. I just couldn't. And I'm glad, in a way, because this was before *Serial* came out and my book would have come out just after *Serial* and I'd have been fucked because *Serial* was so perfect. Well, mainly perfect. Then it hit me that on social media we thought we were going to do things better, and we were actually repeating lots of mistakes that the actual justice system was making.

It's about disproportionate punishment. People do stupid things and they are then disproportionately punished for it. There's just been two incidents in the last couple of days. There was that guy, Tim Hunt, the scientist who went to South Korea and made this speech where he said the problem with women scientists is that (straight away, it's like, 'Shut the fuck up') you fall in love with them and they fall in love with you, and if you criticize them they cry. So he chuckled to himself and got off the stage.

And was fucked.

Of course it was an idiotic thing to say, but now he's been fired, and that's it now, for his career. Because social media demanded it. Obviously what he said doesn't help women scientists, but was his total career destruction the only solution? Not necessarily.

SP: *It has caused us to have far more of a killer instinct in these matters. It's like, 'Right, they need to be sacked, NOW'. Instead of thinking, 'Is this the first time he's done this?' Often without a level of being informed, we're quick to go, 'That person is evil'.*

JR: Yes, you can lead a good ethical life but some bad phraseology in a tweet can overwhelm it. And become a clue to your secret inner evil. Which isn't true about people, by and large. Some people are bad, and their transgressions are so bad that they deserve to be overwhelmed by them. They deserve to be defined by them. But most people aren't like that.

You'd think if it was an isolated incident it could be something he expresses and feels privately regularly, but does that come under our jurisdiction and should it affect what he's doing career-wise?

SP: *The scary thing is it's exciting, because it's free and can be uncorrupted, and really here for the people. But the fact is, we've not all studied journalism and learned fact-checking and source-checking. And again, there are a lot of arguments that the general media has gone a long way from that for a while now, anyway, but still...*

JR: There was another I weighed in on. It was this woman called Rachel Dolezal. She's the head of this Spokane chapter of NAACP [National Association for the Advancement of Colored People] and it turns out she was faking being black. I saw this in the paper and thought, fuck, what a weird, strange, complicated, mysterious story. So I went on Twitter – and, by and large, Twitter wasn't thinking of it as a complicated, fascinating, mysterious story; Twitter was rushing to judge. Some people were being funny about it. But others were being quick to judge, saying 'blackface', 'racist', 'racial appropriation' and so on. And I just thought, it seems to me that this woman's story is complicated and to immediately define her before we know all of the facts is not judicial.

SP: *That's my exact feeling on it: I need to know a bit more. There's no way I can be convinced she is 'right' as such, but it's figuring out how wrong she is.*

JR: And yet within hours of this whole thing happening, everyone felt like they knew her motives: that she was a scheming, cynical, psychopathic liar. She *may* be all those things but when people were yelling those things out at her, no one knew.

This person's life then becomes everybody's plaything, and some people's ideological plaything; for other people it's just something to be funny about, and for others it's just something to scream at. And I just felt that I don't know if I have the stomach for this any more. We know nothing about this woman's life; we know nothing about her. It's obviously fucked up and complicated, but I don't want her to be my plaything. I want her to have some humanity and for people to have compassion. And I said as much on Twitter.

It went down brilliantly. No. You can imagine. Especially because I am a white man. People were saying things like, 'You're a white man. This is not your story.' But that's where I came from. I come from a world where the least you can do is find out about somebody before condemning them.

SP: *You said it exactly right, that waiting is perfectly acceptable.*

JR: The things I'm criticizing social media for, the mainstream media has been doing that stuff for years, too. Turning people into one dimension. I used to do it. I would like to think I haven't done it for a long time. It's what pays well in journalism. And it's wrong. The reason why I feel emotional about it when it happens in social media is because I felt with social media we had the chance to do things better. And I don't think we're really doing anything better. We're making the same mistakes as the mainstream media, we're making the same mistakes as the justice system. We could have created a world of curiosity and instead we've created a world of condemnation. And that's why I weighed in on that woman's story. But it went down badly and I'm turned into a monster. And now I'm just emerging from that.

Somebody – a well-known writer and blogger – wrote 'waiting for Jon Ronson to ever write a piece supporting people of colour, sex-positive people…' I've written for thirty years, writing those pieces. I've really done my time writing about people being abused by power and I feel it's OK for me to also write about people being abused by the power of social media.

You have to constantly prove that you're an appropriate person. That creates a conservative, conformist society, even though we see ourselves as non-conformists. I love Twitter but there's something Adam Curtis said, that the Internet is going to be like one of those John Carpenter movies in the eighties with people shooting and screaming, and people are going to flee to a safer place. Maybe the Internet will go the way of the fucked-up inner city communities of the eighties and people will find a better, calmer, nicer place to live.

SAUL WILLIAMS

Social media, drugs and the connection to the whole

Or, let's look at it openly

SP: *Technology has progressed in a way that the underground can have a worldwide audience and a worldwide reach. There was a point when the underground would have to potentially choose if they were going to dance with the mainstream or not, to get their stuff out there, whereas now you can go, 'No, this is what it is. If it's not welcomed in this format, it will be what it is online and it can reach out in a way still.'*

SW: Exactly. You still have naysayers, and you have tons of people who are like, 'Nah, I can do it this way, and you know what? I can distribute it myself.' Or you can liken it to our relationship to the dark web. We're using the surface web and it's so little of what's possible, to those of us who are not necessarily coding, you know. Like really seeing what's beneath all of this stuff and what we can actually do and how we can actually communicate, and how we can bring new levels to communication. There's a lot available to us.

SP: *Yeah, it's fascinating to think about things like that, that coding and stuff like that in the future will no doubt be an essential part of our children's education. Not in a nerdy 'I can do stuff with computers' way, but in a freedom way. If you learn and understand these things, it will give you that further reach and greater depth to go wherever you want, rather than, 'Here's Google. That's your world: Google and Facebook.'*

SW: It's new tools, like learning how to drive and going from horses to cars. Yeah, there comes a time when the new standard is reached. So even the new definition of literacy is those who are or are not capable of working a computer, really.

SP: *It is a fascinating balance; the Internet and computers and technology should be a huge tool in making progress and making huge progression and jumps, but there's also that fine line between regressing into laziness. If we found ways of not needing to have this any more then that isn't necessarily a bad thing. I'm not necessarily saying spelling, because that's something people get angry about a lot, but there's certain things like language development that have always developed throughout history. If part of that development is through technology, then the focus should be on harnessing that technology and using it in creative ways, rather than saying, 'Your spelling's gone bad.' It's a fine balance, right?*

SW: The most recent epiphany for me has been the interconnectedness that we now achieve through social media, and all of this ability that we have to connect with each other around the world. It makes me think of the movement that happened through drug culture in the sixties, where once again you had these newly forged connections that people felt to the unsaid, the unknown, that made them look at each other and go, 'Yo, fuck the system.'

SP: *And with no preconceived ideas of the negativity of drugs are bad/ drugs are good, just a thing that's new: let's look at it openly.*

SW: This whole turn up, tune up, tune out, all this stuff, and where that led. You'd think of the social movements in France in the sixties – globally in the sixties – you look at all the different social movements that occurred and the thing the youth movements had in common was this new exploration. That exploration was charging them and helping them realize their connectedness to humanity and the greater whole, the shamanic whole. And now, once again, we have this virtual connection. Once again there's the thread of social movements, from the Arab Spring to Occupy to Anonymous and WikiLeaks and Black Lives Matter, all this stuff. The Syrian Electronic Army. You know, there's all this stuff where now we have the ability to connect again. And yeah, we could also talk about addiction; we could also talk about all these things that come about through the connectivity. You see a lot of people exposing parts of themselves that may embarrass you as someone who observes it: 'Oh, why would they say that?'

SP: *It's a fascinating thing if we can look at it with an unbiased mind. I had a doctor on the podcast a while ago, Dr Suzi Gage, and she was talking about studies recently where psychiatrists had been using MDMA in therapy sessions for people with different variations of post-traumatic stress. Because if you take away the social nature of people pilled up, the fact is, this particular drug in its pure form generally makes people just relax and spill their heart out and tell their deepest, darkest secrets. But there is this taboo that these are illegal drugs. Whereas these doctors have gone, 'Wait, we can use this on people struggling to talk about issues they've been through.' They're not saying, 'Take it all the time', but in therapy, in a controlled session.*

SW: Two things: one, I came across that story as well, but what's crazy to me is that when I first heard of MDMA, I heard that it was first used by therapists for couples counselling. So I thought it was already of the understanding or the idea that it came from counselling first, and then reached the streets in the same ways that LSD came from research laboratories of Harvard and what have you. I remember, one of the producers of *Slam* was the founder of *High Times* magazine and he brought me along for an interview with Timothy Leary right before he died, and Timothy Leary was asked, 'If you had one thing that you regret, what would you regret?' And he said, 'I popularized the drug, I didn't popularize the culture that it came from, which in those shamanistic cultures they would take those drugs maybe two to three times in their lifetime, as part of a rites of passage. And now I'm looking at the party usage of this thing and am like, wow, you could have gotten so much more if you'd understood its relationship to a rites of passage and you did it as you entered adulthood and left it there.'

SP: *Completely. More and more people are going and doing Iowaska experiences, where it is a shamanistic thing. Where it's not a 'Well, we're going to get off our faces every weekend and let our hair down.' My experiences, I personally don't do drugs any more, but I've experienced stuff in the past and I feel that LSD is a drug that changed me permanently – not in an 'I'm damaged' way, in an 'I realized some stuff' way. It opened my mind in certain ways, then I could walk away from it; I'd got what I needed from it. Rather than, 'I'm addicted', or the constant use of 'addiction', which is such a loose term: you can be addicted to podcasts, you can be addicted to absolutely anything. There isn't any physical addiction to most of the drugs that are illegal; it's these weird terms and phrases.*

FRANK TURNER

Selfies and social media at gigs

Or, there's art happening here: be part of it

FT: Some of the time Twitter is really frivolous or kind of aggressive, antagonistic, but every now and again something really cool comes through.

SP: *You touched on a thing with Twitter there, I think: people can forget what a great tool it is. And the Internet in general, not to sound like an old man, means you can access everything now, and we underuti-*

lize that hugely. We generally go on there to look at porn or steal music or whatever you choose to do.

FT: Or complain and call someone a twat.

SP: *Yeah. And that's the thing with Twitter, I think. People get angry when people who have a lot of followers complain about abuse and things like that, but I think there's a certain tipping point on Twitter – I'm not there yet – where it loses a lot of its appeal, and not just because of abuse. I chat every now and again with Ed Sheeran, who isn't the most credible name to drop here, but he used to come along to my shows and he's a nice kid, he's huge. So every now and then we'll chat, and that's what exposed me to the fact that people of his size of fame can post the most heart wrenching, true thing and they will get a thousand responses just saying 'follow me' and completely ignoring what's been said. So aside from the fact that you'll also attract a lot of abuse and people who want to hate, even the positive side, even the bit that are your adoring fans, when you get to a certain point they're not there to actually engage and listen to what you're saying. So, you can't even argue that 'Yeah, a few people abuse you but you've got millions of fans.' Yes, but it stops being real, because you've become a product or a badge.*

FT: Well, I think the thing is there are basically only so many people you can have a conversation with at one time. And Twitter is sort of an aggrandized conversation really, or that's what it should be at its best. But if you're Ed Sheeran and you've got a couple of million followers, you can't have a conversation with a couple of million people at the same time, it's not doable. That culture of validation I find pretty depressing as well, do you know what I mean?

SP: *It's bizarre. It makes me feel like an old man because, at points I'll ask people: why do you want me to follow you? Follow is a click of a button. I'm happy to engage and have a conversation with you, surely that should be a bigger goal than the act of following?*

FT: Yeah, completely. And playing shows, I'm sure you get this as well... There was one guy doing it last night, and I don't want to kind of kill the mood by being all schoolmaster-y about it, but there's guys in the front row turning round and taking selfies of themselves. There's a gig happening here, and at its best a gig is a communication; it's a conversation between people; it's a sharing of ideas. It's what art is. And you've completely gone and like stuck a stick in the spokes of all of that because you've made it about you recording yourself being in a certain place.

If you're not interested in watching this person play, which is a completely legitimate thing to feel, there is the entirety of creation minus this little 20-metre-long room in which you could be and exist. There's even just the back of the fucking room. Go and have your conversation there. Right here, there's something happening, there's art happening: be part of it.

RICHARD HERRING

This says more about you than it does about me

Or, why creatives and Twitter trolls have something in common

SP: *You are quite active on Twitter, and I thought you were a very reasoned voice when I was watching the insane unravelling of Andrew Lawrence; when he'd had his rant that was coming across as sexist and racist. I'd seen his stand-up a few times and I still think he's a great writer, a very talented dude. There was instantly this backlash from the left, obviously, just attacking; then him getting defensive and getting more and more offensive. I didn't agree with what he said, but I remember seeing a tweet from you saying, 'Look, we've all had points in our career where we feel we've been ignored for what we're doing, or we deserve this or we deserve that, or someone else is in our place, but you're going about this the wrong way and you're finding villains in "Oh, there has to be a token woman, and women aren't funny" and all this kind of thing'. And I thought it was great to see that medium used in quite a reasoned, calm way.*

RH: Yeah, it was a weird thing. I don't like any point where people start telling – certainly anyone creative – what they can and can't do. And certainly once petitions get into it: I'm really into freedom of speech and I think people should be allowed to say whatever they want. Then, if they're wrong, you can go, 'Look, you're wrong about this, let me tell you why.' And then have a discussion about it. So I think people should be allowed to say anything.

SP: *I'm a big believer that the big wave of e-petitions has killed any value of e-petitions. The fact that there was huge petition to get Glastonbury to change their headliner shows a complete misunderstanding of a business. Glastonbury is its own entity; you can't tell them who they're to book and aren't to book. It's not the BBC. So then I feel it devalues in many ways what was a powerful thing of e-petitions; of being able to petition the BBC or the government or whatever else. When you can petition Andrew Lawrence to shut up, he doesn't have to obey that. Or if we get a thousand names Iain Duncan Smith has to live on a pound a week for a year. That's not how life works!*

RH: I think with Andrew Lawrence I also recognized – not exactly myself in it, because I'd never say the things he said – but the feeling behind it I really understood. Because, you know, you're working hard, you're creating something you're proud of, and it feels like 'Oh why?' But you have to look at the bigger picture, and there are thousands of people trying to create stuff and inevitably some of them aren't going to have their stuff acknowledged in a way it should be acknowledged. It's either good luck, or bad luck. It's that inability to look and think, 'This might be my fault', which a lot of people can't do. I think a lot of creative people can't because a lot of creative people aren't able to question themselves in that way.

It's like a lot of Twitter trolls. If you question why they're doing it, it fucking makes their minds explode. If you say, 'Doesn't this say more about you than it does about me?' They go, 'No! It doesn't! You're rubbish! I'm not going to think about myself!' So it's easy to blame other people for the way your life's going, but you have to take control of it and do your best.

RUFUS HOUND

Recovering from bad Twitter

Or, it's a bit like being burgled

RUFUS HOUND

SP: *What do you see as the positives and negatives of Twitter? I've high-lighted negatives of people complaining about this and that, but both of us are avidly on there so there must be positives that hugely outweigh the negatives, so what's your outlook?*

RH: I feel lots and lots of different things about Twitter. Just to talk about the negatives for a moment; it's a bit like if you've ever been burgled, right? People who've been burgled— And it depends how you've been burgled. Some people have their houses and their lives turned upside down, you know, and it's awful, awful, and I can understand why that would change how you feel about everything. But if you get burgled, and the first thing that happens is you put seventeen locks on every door, and every window's got a security code, actually that means that what those burglars took was more than just your stuff. Whereas you can instead contextually go, well, I'm— in my case— I'm 35 years old. That means that I've lived for whatever 365 times 35 is, that many days, this has happened once, therefore the odds of it happening again are probably one in whatever the 90,000 days I've been alive or whatever that is.

SP: *That makes sense.*

RH: So, OK, that was a bit of bad luck. There are some desperate people in the world. Oh well, take sensible precautions, remember to lock up and if that door wasn't strong enough maybe get a slightly stronger door, but I'm not going to now live in Colditz because that happened. That's sort of how I feel a little bit about Twitter.

What keeps happening to me on Twitter is I'll post something that I know is fairly innocuous, but somebody will take offence at some part of it and, even as I'm writing it, I know the people who are going to take offence. So it feels like the onus slightly becomes to accept that there are now so many users of Twitter that anything you write, somebody somewhere is going to take offence, and actually the more followers you have, the higher the inevitability of that.

SP: *In fact, if no one takes offence, you're in Westlife/James Blunt territory with your tweets.*

RH: Although, James Blunt: brilliant at Twitter.

SP: *Absolutely genius at Twitter. One of the funniest. I mean, we don't need to plug him any more, everyone seems to know about this, but he's very, very funny.*

RH: Very good at Twitter, and actually a real lesson in how to take those things with a pinch of salt and play them with grace.

SP: *Definitely.*

RH: So, there's a bit of that. Obviously I've made quite a lot of noise about the stealth privatization of the NHS. Well, the nurses all went on strike and that morning I did half a dozen tweets saying support the nurses, solidarity with the nurses, they're out there. You know, 'If you're going past a hospital today and see those people outside, you have to know that this isn't because they themselves want more. It's because they've had what little they had taken away from them and they're just trying to get a little bit of it back.' And those were all the messages I was sending out that morning.

There were storms everywhere that day and all these women are out there – it's mainly women in nursing, not exclusively, but mainly – in this pouring rain. You know, standing up for what's right and what they're owed. And obviously the dopey version of that was, 'Mind you, upside – it's like the UK's biggest ever wet T-shirt competition, right?' Which is obviously a joke of, 'Oh, there's an upside to these poor, like, compassionate, brilliant professionals having to stand in the freezing cold rain. Oh, that's funny isn't it. Ha, ha, laugh at them.' No! Because I've spent all morning saying that that isn't it.

SP: *That's the scary part of Twitter: the ability to take one tweet and retweet that to your followers and therefore it be completely out of context and horrible. I had a big argument on Twitter one time with someone; it was an argument over women's rights, and they'd misunderstood something I'd said. I'm always up for a reasoned discussion, I don't get angry easily – if I'm wrong, I'm happy to be wrong. I'm regularly wrong, I love to learn through being wrong and learn from other people.*

RH: Which is an open-mindedness which I do not think people are really being told is the only way to live. Everybody grows up, is given one opinion and it becomes: 'I'm going to stick to that till the day I die.' 'What if you're wrong?' 'I'm NOT WRONG!'

SP: *It's how it should be. The thing that in this instance pushed me over the edge was that, while we're having this discussion – in which I conceded where I was wrong and she conceded where she'd misinterpreted – I suddenly started to notice that she was retweeting only my tweets that, out of context, made me look bad, and I found that hugely unfair. And I got a bit angry but then just said, 'Look, I'm going to end this conversation.'*

She was known as an activist for women's rights so, again, she was someone I didn't want to be having an argument with, because I support everything she does essentially. But she was putting across an inaccurate portrayal of our conversation and I think it's equally damaging. I talk about this quite a lot, but it's equally damaging to poorly report stuff on the left, for example, as it is the idiots on Fox who report that Birmingham is a Muslim-only city. If anything it's more damaging, because then it discredits everything.

RH: Because that's their game, and we're going to inspire by getting our game strong.

SP: *Yeah, exactly. It's the same as people complaining to the BBC about shows that they've not seen but they've seen a quote out of context. It's that exact same thing. So that's where it's kind of a scary and weird thing, I guess.*

RH: Do you know the American comic Patton Oswalt?

SP: *Yes, yes.*

RH: Going back a couple of years now, he did a series of brilliant tweets and I'm very hamfistedly going to quote them, but you'll get the gist. People were retweeting stuff from Patton Oswalt that appeared to be saying: gay people need to get out of this country, they're dragging the economy down and perverting the true sense of what it is to be American. These tweets had clearly come from Patton Oswalt's account, and there were things like 'Muslims need to go home', and all this kind of stuff. And you think, holy shit. What he was doing was deliberately sending two tweets, where the first was, 'You know something, I'm absolutely sick to the back teeth of these fucking idiots who spend all their time on Twitter saying bullshit like...' Then the second tweet would be all of these homophobic raves. But that makes the point: without context, without seeing what else was written, the very worst thing that could be said looks like it could be being said.

SP: *So really Twitter essentially has one of the biggest crosses to bear that stand-up and comedy have had for years; of people taking individual lines and not putting them in the context of an hour-long set, or a 20-minute piece that has built to this specific line. And you see people in court cases reading out sections of stand-up sets. It's like, I'm sorry — you're not qualified to perform this material.*

RH: Have you seen that video of Emily Maitlis repeating Frankie Boyle jokes to Mark Thompson, when he was director-general, on *Newsnight*? He's like, 'Emily, listen...'

SP: *Your timing's off, your tone's wrong.*

RH: You've got to say it with charm. That is it. What is genuinely funny in a comedy club on a Saturday night is not funny on a Monday morning over your cornflakes, as put through the filter of *Daily Mail* reportage.

SIMON PEGG

What's it all for?

Or, having a Zoolander moment

SPegg: The best thing the Internet ever did was give everybody a voice, and the worst thing the Internet did was give everybody a voice.

SP: *It does make you realize there are a lot of idiots. You think, 'Oh really? That's not the voice I hoped the Internet would have.'*

SPegg: The unfortunate thing is that it's kind of democratized the worst things about people. Because it's enabled people who would ordinarily keep their bitterness to themselves to find community in that negativity. There's a word now – 'hater' – for a person who is just predisposed to hating, and it's a shame in a way because I feel like it's legitimized a lot of bad things.

SP: *I think the invention of haters is horrible for there being the idea of a hater, but then it also allows people to have the illusion that if anyone legitimately criticizes something, that they're a hater. Sometimes you need to hear critical stuff; sometimes it's good to hear that. It's now easy to go, 'Ah, haters.' But maybe they're not? Maybe you need to take a lesson from that.*

SPegg: That's true. It does cloud the field of constructive criticism because you can dismiss it as being hubris when there might actually be valid points out there.

SP: *Always interesting. Do you spend a lot of time online? Are you an Internet fan? That sounds like a ridiculous question... But a lot of people avoid it. A lot of people in the public eye will choose to preserve their own creativity by avoiding it. Do you embrace it?*

SPegg: I am an Internet fan. I just recently left Twitter. I deleted my Twitter and— I had a good five years but I started to question it more and more because I just suddenly thought… I had a bit of a *Zoolander* moment where I just thought, 'Who am I?' I was looking into a puddle and saw my reflection, and I thought, 'Why am I doing this?'

Because what I want to be is an actor. I try very hard in other areas of my life not to be a celebrity and having to do press you do sometimes have to go to events and stuff; it's a part of the thing. But if you don't seek it out you can preserve a little bit of yourself; whereas Twitter is a sort of personal celebrity generator. You can create your own celebrity one person at a time, and I think, for an actor, I thought suddenly: I shouldn't be doing this.

What I thought initially was, oh, if I have a film coming out I can use it as a promotional thing. But even that would feel like, oh Jesus, I'm really hammering this, people are going to be really bored of this. But when I have a film come out, I want people to think, oh I haven't seen him for a while, I wonder what he's been up to? Not, I know what he had for breakfast this morning.

SP: *Yes, it's easy to forget that everyone on Twitter is just a person and everyone in the films is just a person; so it's easy for you to forget you're not just a person, that you're an actor, that you're this thing. A friend of mine – Flux Pavilion, a musician and producer – he had a similar realization: 'I make music and I've just posted about popping down to the shop for something. That's not relevant in any way to my music.'*

If you feel it can lend to something else, then that's legitimate. But you forget that you're talking and treating it like it's just your friends who are on Facebook or Twitter or whatever, but that's not who you are; you have a public persona as well. You've got to choose whether you want to share that or not.

SPegg: Yeah, I didn't leave because I thought Twitter was rubbish. I totally get the value of it and for some people it's necessary. If you're a stand-up comedian – and I think this is where I kind of got into trouble – and your bread and butter is getting people to find what you say funny and come and see you, then it's great in a way because you can make jokes on it, you can publicize your tours or whatever. Because that's what your job is: to be that person. Often stand-up comedians, unless they play characters, are generally themselves telling jokes. It is very worthwhile for a lot of people, but for me, I started to get a little uncomfortable with the degree of narcissism involved in Twitter. I started to think, who gives a fuck what I say? When people started dying— I know that started a long time ago...

SP: *Yeah it's been around a while, pre-Internet.*

SPegg: Yeah, it's popular. It is pre-Internet. When someone died that I knew or that I respected you'd feel compelled to write a little 140-character obit: 'Sad to see them go,' whatever. And then... Every now and then Sky News would run it and I was sitting there thinking, does everything have to be shone through the prism of famous people? How does that legitimize anything?

SP: *I love Twitter but I am aware of the negative side – and one of the great negatives about it is that it has become, or can be referred to now, as journalism. Which is disgusting. The fact that people will report: 'Here's a news story.' And I'll think, I know that news story because that was a tweet, and you've written a whole article about a 140-character tweet. You've padded that out and that's been your research for today; that's been your journalism. You've got up and looked on Twitter.*

SPegg: It's become a resource for journalists to just crib quotes. And particularly when it's about someone who's died. I started to feel like... I saw someone had died and said very honestly – and not thinking, I hope someone picks up on this – 'I'm very sorry to see them go.' And I saw it picked up in the paper and I was furious because I thought, I didn't put it on there for that. I remember when Rik Mayall died, which was terribly upsetting because I'd worked with him, he was my hero as a kid; I loved him dearly. I remember agonizing over what to do, because I couldn't say nothing, I had to say something, but I didn't want to write something that could be picked up on.

SP: *It's such an odd situation because it's a self-imposed situation, a self-inflicted thing: you've chosen to be on this media network and now...*

SPegg: I remember I was talking about something once; I'd tweeted some asinine comment about something, and somebody tweeted, 'Don't you know Brittany Murphy just died?' No, I didn't actually. And I was lambasted for not making a comment.

SP: *I've had the same. I've had issues before tweeting stuff and not having read the papers, and then stuff can seem to be related and it's not, it's completely unrelated.*

SPegg: I went to a T-shirt shop in Vancouver called Bang on the morning of the Boston bombing and I tweeted a thing about 'Just popped into Bang, amazing, blah blah blah'. And I got so much anger from people going, 'How dare you? That's so insensitive.' And I genuinely hadn't seen the story. And even when I did see the story I felt, wait a minute, that's a little unfair.

SP: *And then it's weird – you're having to think, should I argue this? Why are you having to have that inner conversation? 'I don't think that is wrong...' It's so beside the point.*

ZANE LOWE

The algorithm of the modern age

Or, you just need not to fight this

SP: *You were one of the first people I saw to really engage that live audience on social media.*

ZL: It's funny, I may have been one of the first, or at the beginning – with DJs – to try to incorporate it into radio, but I was late with social media. I didn't really want to use Facebook; I didn't really want to do that. I was like 'Nah', you know? I remember Annie Mac saying, 'You on Twitter?' And I was like, 'What the hell is Twitter?!' And she said,

'Man, I've got 26,000 followers on Twitter.' And I was quite belligerent about it.

I had this thing in my mind of, 'Ah man, whatever.' Couldn't have been more wrong. I remember – I'm just going to say it because I've never really said who it was – but I remember having two hangouts with two different artists and both of them giving me a hard time about it within about a month of each other, completely unrelated.

I remember having a coffee with Mike Skinner and he said, 'You need to get on Twitter. You need to get on Twitter, because I want to hear what you have to say on Twitter, and secondly, if you don't, you're going to get left behind. Because at some point, people are going to start measuring part of your worth according to how many people you can reach on these things.'

Mike's a very smart guy, so I thought I'd listen to him. So that planted the seed. Then I was in LA and, just through mutual friends, I ended up having dinner with a bunch of people and one of them was Trent Reznor. So I'm sitting opposite Trent Reznor – and me and Trent get on really good now, but this was one of the first times we met, properly – and he was just like, 'How are you?' I'd had this disastrous run of TV meetings in LA and nothing had come of it because they wanted panel shows; they wanted the next *American Idol* guys and I'm not that, and I said, 'It's been disastrous.' And he went, 'Well, you should use the Internet more. And stop worrying about where you've been and start worrying about where you're going.'

And this just made me think: OK if these two guys, who are two of the smartest people I've ever listened to...

SP: *Trent, in particular, you probably wouldn't think of him as an advocate of social media.*

ZL: He was really big on it at the beginning, at the time. But the funny thing was, within two months of them telling me that, and I'd started my account, they'd both fucked off! They'd both walked away for like a year each. Thanks guys, what did you walk me into?!

SP: *They wanted to leave it in safe hands – 'We both want to leave, we need to get someone to look after this shit while we're gone.'*

ZL: I think they'd both just had enough for a while, but by that point I realized this is a thing I needed to get on. Then I started to incorporate it into the radio. 'Look, this is how we're going to measure the connectability. And also, we can really connect to the audience in real time. And we can also canvas for listeners. It sounds awfully political and horrible but we can go online and we can link a band. Put the link up to the radio station online and we can say, "Coming up next is this." And immediately the band are going to retweet to all their fans. And if you can get a hundred people tuning in off that then you're connecting to more people.' So I was like, this is so straightforward and the fact that I've been so slow on this is something I'll only ever admit to Scroobius Pip.

SP: *It makes tons of sense, though. And it really works with the live show and the interactive news. And the thing with live radio, the buzz when you're doing it, is about connection with other people. Playing that track and not just sitting there and going, 'I've played it, that's out there.' Just seeing the excitement that you got coming back at you.*

ZL: Well we were faced with this Internet revolution when I was still on the air and all of a sudden songs were leaking and, 'Hang on, when are we playing this song? How's this working? Where's our cornerstone philosophy of getting the music to you as quickly as we can, and we're supposed to break records so how are we going to...?' Again, I got some really great advice, which was, 'You just need not to fight this, because, by the way, every industry is going to be affected by this. So don't just think you're a hard-done-by music fan. It's gonna happen. This is the on-demand future and it's about to go down. So you just need to adapt and make it work for you.'

So that's what we did and we started to loosen up and let go, and just actually work with the Internet and use it. And I suddenly realized, I don't want to be blasting people with hashtags the whole time. What I want to be doing is using the Internet silently for the show. So not make it a radio feature, just use it for what it's there for. Use it parallel, alongside the radio show, and integrate it quietly rather than just, 'I'm online, check out this, and this, and that.' No, I'll just be online while I'm on the air and if you are too, then great.

Here's something that's going to happen: we're entering into a playlist future, which is playlist present. That's great; we all make playlists, we're into it, but the thing about algorithms is algorithms don't sell music to people: they make it available. But within an hour something else is the story. So you have an hour window where you're trending: 'This song's leaked, oh my God.' Then an hour later something else has taken its place and who knows if in that hour it's caught. You'll know in a week if it's got hundreds of millions of listens but it just might not catch.

What the heart affords us is real rhythm, so if you can combine the two – the algorithm of the modern age with the real rhythm of human endorsement, a real passion – then that to me is where we're at.

SP: *Completely. I've always felt that a recommendation from a friend is worth a million times more than a play on whatever platform.*

ZL: That's how you get into music. That's how you learn. You either learn it from your parents or you learn it from your siblings or you learn it from the guy behind the record counter, back in the day. Or from your friends at school. Or because someone's wearing a T-shirt and it looks cool and you want to know what that is. You won't learn so much if it just shows up on a playlist, because what is it? Where's the story? Where's the romance of it? Where's the mystery, where's the excitement, where's the build? I don't know, man. I'm all for pushing forward and progressing – I'm very progressively minded now, but at the same time, I know that human beings need to communicate with human beings.

5

MENTAL HEALTH

As the *Distraction Pieces* podcast grew it was interesting to see which subjects seemed to come up again and again. Now, a few years back, while I was sat at the Sony Awards waiting for them to announce the winner of the category that I was nominated in, they started to describe the unnamed winner. They used the term 'non-linear maverick', and at that point my producer, Dan Riedo, and I looked at each other and, for the first time, realized we may have won. You see, 'non-linear maverick' is a cool-sounding way of saying 'making it up as he goes along, showing no sign of a plan or structure', which felt like it HAD to be talking about my show at the time, the Beatdown. (They were, we won, and I forgot to thank Dan Riedo, who was literally next to me and worked on every single episode... Not my proudest moment.)

Anyway, the reason I mention this is because it kind of tells you a lot about how these podcasts tend to go. While I prepare notes and have topics I hope to get round to, they often don't get looked at and any structure goes out the window pretty quickly. That's why it was so surprising when the same things kept coming up.

What that told me, quite quickly, is that, while the subject of mental health seems to still be quite taboo in this country, it's something that affects pretty much all of us. I have been lucky to have people like Eddy Temple-Morris, Gail Porter, Tom Robinson and more be impossibly open about their own struggles over the years, and it is those episodes that have had some of the deepest reactions.

To this day, not a week goes by when I don't get a tweet or message from someone who has just found either Eddy's episode or Gail's and has been so moved by it they simply had to get in touch.

Now, mental health is a truly delicate thing, and something that's very hard to understand, due to its personal and individual nature. But having open discussions about it is key for us to stop burying these things or thinking they're wrong. The thought that people should be ashamed of struggling in life at times really needs to be put to bed. It's the most human thing in the world!

Equally, I feel we can over-label things at times and end up making them even worse than they are. Let me pour my heart out with an example here. There was a time recently when I was very down. I buried myself in work and didn't interact with friends too much as my own way of coping with it. But, you know what? I don't feel I was 'depressed'. The fact of the matter is, I had some really unpleasant stuff going on in my life, which made me sad. And that's totally normal and OK.

When we go through painful experiences, it's fine to feel sad. It shouldn't be something we feel ashamed of or guilty about. In our lives we will, and even SHOULD, feel a wide range of emotions. Not all of them will be enjoyable, but I truly believe they all help us grow in some way.

We put such pressure on always wishing to be happy (automatic smiles in every photo, social media competition for the happiest life) that we forget it isn't the ONLY emotion out there.

I mean, make no mistake, it's a GREAT one. A solid rank in the top five all-time best emotions, without a doubt. But there are other emotions, too, and we will all encounter them at some point in our lives, and that's absolutely fine.

DR SUZI GAGE

The drugs might work

Or, but still, don't try this at home

SP: *Let's talk about the studies in London at the moment that are looking at the use of what are traditionally recreational drugs as treatments for depression, for PTSD, for all sorts of other things.*

SG: Dr Robin Carhart-Harris was presenting his work and it's very much a pilot study at the moment but they're using psilocybin – the active ingredient in magic mushrooms – to try to help people with treatment-resistant depression. So these are people who've tried many different kinds of drugs or different non-drug therapies for their depression and nothing has worked. So they're trying to use psilocybin in quite high doses just once or twice, to see if that can work as sort of a reset. Because a lot of people, when they take psilocybin, report these gnostic or spiritual experiences and describe it as the dissolution of the ego, taking away the self. But as well as anecdotal reports about the effects, they've also looked at brain scans, so neural networks within the brain. What tends to happen when you're on psychedelics, they've found from these studies, is the individual brain networks fire less, and there are many more global connections firing in the brain, which is really interesting to observe. And you do see the opposite patterns in patients with depression. So that's another reason you might think psychedelics might be a good avenue to go down.

SP: *It's a fascinating one at the moment – as you were saying about the treatment, doing it as a one-off, as a reset. I don't do anything at the moment, but in the past I've used hallucinogens. And again, I need to preface this with the statement that I don't think anyone can say, 'I've done this, therefore it's safe.' I think it's as we've said on all of these things: it's such a personal thing. For some people it's incredibly dangerous, for others, it's not at all. But my experience of hallucinogens changed me permanently: it opened up certain parts of my mind and philosophies and outlooks to me that have stuck with me since. I can completely understand how that could be a similar thing in depression or mental health issues where it can have that moment: it could potentially be a one-off treatment to click the reset button, essentially.*

SG: What I should note very quickly is that when they do these studies in Imperial, it's always in a therapeutic environment. So it's very, very different to going to some person on a street corner and taking something where you don't know what it is.

SP: *The safety of it, of knowing what you've got and the controlled environment makes all the difference. It's one of the main arguments for decriminalization; the control over the quality and the situation and who's taking them. Just so that's clear: the studies aren't buying off Weird*

Bobby up the street then doing them in someone's back garden. It's the purity, taking specific parts of these hallucinogens, then testing that in a controlled environment.

SG: Yeah, absolutely. And similarly with the PTSD trials in the States and MDMA. The theory behind MDMA being used in PTSD trials is that the type of feeling that you have on MDMA is that you are able to confront unpleasant memories without the fear response that you associate with them: it's putting yourself in a safe place. So you can see how in a talking therapy session, to be in a place where you feel able to talk about memories that at that moment you can't talk about without triggering horrible stress responses, that that could be a really useful way of progressing the therapy session and getting you able to confront these in an environment where you feel safe.

SP: *That's fascinating. Again; in the controlled situation and the purity. The biggest risk of things like MDMA and pills in that kind of area is what they're all cut with and mixed with – all the other horrible things that are in there.*

SG: MDMA was originally made as a by-product while trying to make a blood-thinning drug, way back in the early 1900s, maybe 1920s.

SP: *Wow, I was ready for you to say sixties or seventies.*

SG: In the seventies Alexander Shulgin heard about it, and him and his friends – quite a lot of whom were psychotherapists – they used to use it in their counselling, but they also used to use it recreationally. I think he used to refer to it as his low-calorie Martini.

SP: *Oh, the ignorance of history!*

SG: Well, the Royal physician to Queen Victoria used to prescribe tincture of cannabis for childbirth pains to his patients. It's very interesting the drugs that have become the recreational drugs of choice, the legal ones, compared to the ones that are now illegal. That's a whole different story, perhaps!

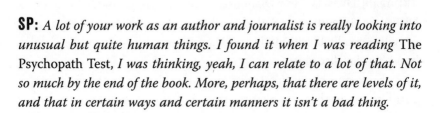

JON RONSON

We're all psychopaths

Or, the power of diagnosis

SP: *A lot of your work as an author and journalist is really looking into unusual but quite human things. I found it when I was reading* The Psychopath Test, *I was thinking, yeah, I can relate to a lot of that. Not so much by the end of the book. More, perhaps, that there are levels of it, and that in certain ways and certain manners it isn't a bad thing.*

JR: There is a line in *The Psychopath Test* where a psychiatrist says, 'If you're worried if you're a psychopath, then you're not one.' Sometimes I wish I were a bit more psychopathic; it would make me feel less anxious, because anxiety is the opposite of psychopathy. That is something I wish I wasn't in my life. Yet if I take a Xanax I feel groggy. And I think I'd rather feel anxious than groggy.

So I just got mired in my psychopath-spotting abilities. There was a woman on Twitter causing me some trouble, a bit stalkery, and I was a bit alarmed by it. I talked to an eminent psychiatrist who's involved in the psychopath field and I told him a couple of things she'd said, and he said, 'Definitely a psychopath. No question.' And I said, 'Yeah, definitely.' And she's not! She's a delightful young lady. And this was someone with the power of diagnosis. Obviously he was saying it informally in an interview situation, he wasn't about to lock her up. I don't put any of that in the book. That was when I thought maybe having that power of diagnosis can turn you a bit psychopathic.

SP: *That was another thing that instantly drew me to* The Psychopath Test: *my favourite film is* Harvey. *It's bizarrely become so relevant again because of the over-diagnosis of everything. There's a lot toward the start (of* The Psychopath Test) *about over-medication, particularly in America.*

JR: In the States, girls as young as two and three are getting diagnosed with bipolar. It's not happening quite so much now because there were deaths [from over-prescribing], but it took deaths to make it stop. They were getting diagnosed as bipolar because they had temper tantrums.

SP: *It was amazing how big the book had become of different things you can be diagnosed for.*

JR: Yeah, DSM-IV [the Diagnostic and Statistical Manual of Mental Disorders, 4th edition] is 850 pages. DSM-V is even bigger. There's even something called 'arithmetic learning disorder'. They got rid of childhood bipolar disorder.

I think one shouldn't throw out the baby with the bath water. I still maintain that some labelling and diagnoses can help, and some medications help some people in some situations, so I'm not going all RD Laing here. I did notice that there were really extreme positions. If you don't believe in the DSM you're a crazy Scientologist. On the other side, the mental health deniers will say there's no such thing as an anxiety disorder, it's just not true. And obviously the truth lies in the unfashionable grey area, in the middle.

GAIL PORTER

Happiness ain't all that

Or, the demonization of every experience
that isn't happiness

SP: *Do you think there is such a thing as healthy depression? That's a term I've just invented there, but just talking to you about some of the things you go through, if people calm the fuck down and leave you to it, it's not a bad thing entirely...*

GP: I think I understand.

SP: *It really is important to let people know that you are there to talk to them, but at points you don't want or require that.*

GP: I think I get where you say healthy depression. There are times where I have bad days, but it also makes me think about things and think about other people and think about where I'm at. You can be sad and feel a bit dark but your brain is always working, and I always try to get something from it. If I'm writing, sometimes I'll look back when I'm having dark days and think, fuck. I'll read something I've written four days later and it's like two different people. I'd get angry with myself and think, that doesn't flow, but then I'd think, well, hang on a minute, I don't flow, and I'm quite happy with me at the minute. I've gone through enough. You go up, you go down…

SP: *I couldn't agree more. Whenever I word it or say it out loud I sound ridiculous. But in our society in general we put far too much importance on happiness being the only goal. If we're not happy then everything is shit. Happiness is awesome, but there's also intellectual fulfilment. Even sadness and anger – they're important things to go through and experience.*

GP: Yeah, it makes you the person you are.

SP: *You can't feel you're failing because you're not particularly cheery one week.*

GP: Look at some of the great artists and songwriters and poets… They're all over the place. And comedians; they're not happy all of the time. Most of them are manic depressives. I did a walk up mountains with a team from Mind, and every single person on my team had all suffered from depression, anxiety, whatever else. Everyone was perfect, in my eyes. Everyone had their own stories. Some people had been through stuff you could not even imagine, and yet we're all up there on a mountain, laughing, talking about it, and you think, how did they come out the other end? And they were sending me messages afterwards going, 'How did you do it? You're inspirational.' And I'd go, 'No, you're inspirational!' So we've all got our bits and pieces.

SP: *It's weird; it's the demonization of every experience that isn't happiness.*

GP: Yeah, and what's normal?

SP: *Like you said, you just got through it the way you believe a normal person would. But because everyone who hasn't experienced it is like, 'Man, that's the most horrible thing.' No, it's bad, but stuff happens and you adapt and go on with it.*

GP: You either give up or keep going. It's not that easy for everyone; obviously there are a lot of people who can't get out. I've been in a rut where I thought I was never going to get out of it and I was sectioned. And then I thought I was never going to get out of that either, because that was just horrific. But then I had the strength, wherever it came from, to think, I've got to pull myself out of it. I think it came from my daughter. But I can totally get how someone could get to a really a dark place and not have anything that they have to grasp on to or someone they love so much it keeps them going.

SP: *We talked about how sometimes it's OK not to want to talk to people. I wanted to say, however, it is important to talk and there are people like CALM [Campaign Against Living Miserably] and Mind and the Samaritans. My mum's worked with the Samaritans for years. It blew me away that they're not allowed to try and talk you out of anything. That made them appeal to me more, because it's a non-judgemental thing then. If you choose to ring up and say, 'Right, I've got to the end of my tether,' then you're not going to be judged, even for that. Hopefully it wouldn't be the case: in general, you're talking to someone and it will change.*

GP: Yeah, I've spoken to the Samaritans. I've been through it for on and off 20-odd years – 25 years – I've been really struggling. But now I've got to a place that I know what makes me happier, when I'm in a really bad stage – who to talk to and who not to – and I know when I want to be on my own. But there are a lot of times, even if you think you want to be on your own and you're struggling, you have to talk to someone.

EDDY TEMPLE-MORRIS

Standing down from manning up

Or, we all need to offload

SP: *We've both worked a lot with CALM, a charity trying to address the fact that the highest killer of males between 18 and 47 is suicide in the UK. Men have a problem talking about these things.*

ETM: I'm the chair of their music board and I got involved with them, as everybody that gets involved with CALM does, because of a personal thing.

SP: *I think where there's a personal investment it means all the more.*

ETM: What I find unacceptable is that you and I are four times more likely to kill ourselves than our mum, our sister or our girlfriend. And that's just unacceptable. And this whole 'man up' thing.

I've had several people over the years who have taken their own lives, but the one that hit me the hardest and most profoundly was just horrible the way I found out about it. I was actually live on air doing my show on Xfm and I was playing a mix of Losers songs – the band I'm honoured to play for. I was just queuing up an Ou Est le Swimming Pool track, when suddenly I get a ton of messages saying, 'Eddy, Eddy, Eddy – have you not heard?' So I'm playing the record then the news comes in that dear Charlie [Haddon, of Ou Est le Swimming Pool] had taken his own life at Pukkelpop festival. And the whole horror of it unfolded while I was live on air. I just had to deal with it right there and then. It was awful.

Instead of an album launch, they got different bands to each do a cover of the songs on the album and linked them all together at Koko. It was there I got to meet this amazing woman, Jane Powell, who runs CALM. She said to me then, 'What's the biggest killer of young men in this country.' I said, 'Surely it's drugs?' She said, 'No.' And I said, 'Well, car crashes, bike crashes?' She said, 'No. If you added cars, bikes and drugs together you wouldn't even touch it – it's actually the men themselves.' That blew me away. Then she explained she ran this charity and they had so little money that she couldn't afford to put a stamp on an envelope after getting a message from the police in Liverpool who were saying, 'We've got all these kids dropping like flies and what do we do?' And she couldn't afford a stamp to put on an envelope to send them some literature. They couldn't afford to have a phone line or anything like that, certainly not one that is open all the time.

So I just started fundraising and raising awareness for them. And you know, through the support of people like you, it's got a lot better. The awareness has gone through the roof on this issue.

SP: *It really has, and it's building. I lost a dear friend who took his own life and I thank him in everything I release because I felt a pressure to work harder and do better because he wasn't around. We were into the same music and same stuff so it was a strange motivation in that respect. But I find it fascinating that there is any taboo whatsoever over counselling or over seeking help or over talking to people. It blows my mind that there is this strong silent thing or stiff upper lip in Britain still. It's ridiculous because people don't realize we're not designed – and never have been – to handle the trials and tribulations of life on our own. Cave men had communities and there were far more people helping each other out. You'd go to the shaman for advice on what the future holds; that's counselling, not knowing what your future is. Yet we see it as a weakness to seek help and to seek advice, which is one of the oldest things in human history. You think of the toughest people you can think of – cave men and Vikings – they would all go to elders for advice. We don't have that in communities now, so the equivalent is trained counsellors – people like CALM, people like the Samaritans.*

It would be great if there was one universal number to call, in the same way as there is 999 if you've got an emergency – a number you could call about domestic violence, abuse, depression, suicidal thoughts – so you could have that access.

ETM: It's so simple. Nobody kills themself while they're talking to someone.

SP: *People don't realize how powerful the act of talking and saying stuff out loud is, and offloading.*

ETM: I tell you what I found incredibly interesting, Pip. When I hit rock bottom at the end of 2013, I got into a situation where I had a suicide plan. I wanted to die, plain and simple, and I knew how I was going to do it. I knew where I was going to park my car, and I had this whole thing. I'm one of these often annoying people when someone says, 'How are you?' I offload, straight away. It happened on the steps outside of this studio – this lovely guy, Neil, goes, 'How are you man?' I went, 'Shit, absolutely shit.' And he was absolutely stunned, like, 'I was only being nice.' I remember feeling just awful that he had made such a nice gesture but he was obviously expecting the stock male response of, 'I'm fine, thanks.' But I wasn't. So I said I wasn't.

I sent him an email just saying, 'Mate, I'm so sorry I did that. I'm having some real problems at the moment and I'm just very honest. I'm brutally honest sometimes and I'm very sorry that your nice gesture wasn't returned in the spirit with which it was given.' He was so nice, he sent me such a lovely email back. Friends would say, 'How are you?' I'd say, 'Really bad.' They'd say, 'Why?' And I'd talk about my own mental health. And I found out, horrifically, that about nine out of ten of the men I talked to had either tried to commit suicide or were on happy pills or had been on happy pills or been depressed or walked into A&E thinking they were insane – all these things that had happened to me. It was just staggering the amount of people out there who have mental health issues but then don't talk about it.

SP: *And it's so important to know how regular and human it is to have these worries and to get into these places. The fact you are someone who had worked with CALM, who knew about all of this, and you still found yourself at that point. It's not like you were ignorant; you were aware of the pitfalls. So the fact you found yourself in that situation means it's so regular for anyone to find themself in that way. And equally it's so achievable to pull themself out, despite it not seeming clear at the time. There is that light at the end of the tunnel.*

BLINDBOY

The ugly game of fame

Or, it's an unfillable hole

SP: *I remember the first time I saw Rubberbandits: before I heard you guys, I fell in love with the image of you with plastic bags on your heads. I thought it was a very striking image.*

BB: The thing with the bag, I suppose, is just a rejection of celebrity bullshit, do you know what I mean? We grew up watching *Big Brother*. And *Big Brother*, when it started, you'd have people who won the competition and for a week they're the most famous person in Britain and Ireland, then they slowly fade. And it confronted us with the fact that, Jesus Christ, celebrity isn't all that nice. Being recognized probably isn't all that nice. D'you know? So we adopted the bags. I get to casually buy carrots in Aldi and no one bothers me.

SP: *On the whole celebrity thing,* Big Brother *is one thing: the fact is, you've prepared for that, for probably a month. You've probably thought, I'll put my application in, do it, have my moment, then you drop off. The one that gets me, though, is the Olympics. You'll train for four years – or your whole life – but there will be four years building up to the Olympics. Even if you win gold, probably a week later, you can walk down the street and no one's going to give a shit. It's a bizarre one. For the briefest moment it's the biggest thing in the world, and people will train years and years for it, and then you could— we could have walked past several Olympic gold medallists on the way here and not known.*

BB: What does that do to a person's self-esteem? The thing is, every human thinks they want fame but once you get it, it's a quite a negative thing. It's not good for a person's self-esteem to be receiving too much external praise, because if everybody is saying, 'You're brilliant, you're brilliant, you're brilliant,' the person starts to believe it themselves. I think personally it's what got to Kurt Cobain. Kurt Cobain was a man with a lot of mental issues and a lot of self-esteem issues. And the world was telling him he was brilliant, but he inside was telling himself he was shit. 'I'm going to be found out, I'm going to be exposed.' When people would say to him, '"Teen Spirit" is an incredible song.' He himself would go, 'It's not, I just stole "More Than a Feeling" by Boston.' He didn't actually have the self-esteem to appreciate his own creativity. It was a self-loathing thing. And he didn't end up in a very nice situation.

SP: *It's interesting. You're right there. It's as much that we're told we all want fame and we're all craving fame. In this brief conversation I've solved that Olympic thing – they probably don't give a fuck about fame. That's not why they're doing it.*

BB: No, it's a different goal.

SP: *They're doing it for that achievement. I've got a guy on the label called Jackamo Brown who's a folk singer. He had an album and it got seven or eight out of ten in* Uncut *magazine, and it's had good reviews – it was a debut album so we didn't expect to get any coverage. He hasn't done anything since, because he never had any desire to be famous as a musician. He played two live gigs, he didn't see the appeal, and just put a record out. People always hit me up asking, 'When's his next album?' I don't think he's working on anything; he just had some songs and recorded them. I twisted his arm into putting them out. So it's kind of a beautiful thing but it shocks you. People are shocked when I say that. It's just, 'Well no, he just isn't into it.' But we assume everyone's goal is to be famous.*

BB: I think it's a lack of self-love, a lack of self-compassion. Everyone has that issue. Look at the nature of our society. We live in a consumerist society and advertising only functions by keeping us down. I can't remember the last time I've been sold a bar of soap based on how clean it's going to make me. I'm sold a bar of soap based on how thin it's going to make me or how beautiful it's going to make me. Our entire consumer culture needs us to have a low level of self-esteem, or self-love. So everyone thinks, if I get this approval from everybody, it'll be OK. And it's not the case.

Unless you've got an empathic relationship with your own emotions, or you've got a degree of self-love, it doesn't matter how many people tell you that you are brilliant. It's never going to be enough. Never ever ever. Because it's an unfillable hole. Addiction as well – with people who are in the public eye. There's the argument if somebody's famous they're more exposed to drugs at parties. Here's the other thing about it, if I didn't have a bag on my head, I wouldn't be able to walk into a pub in Ireland without someone either calling me a cunt or buying me a pint. One or the other. And there was an Irish folk musician called Luke Kelly who turned into a very desperate alcoholic. He himself said the reason he became an alcoholic – he wasn't even interested that much in drinking – was people assumed he was, because he played Irish folk music. He couldn't stop having pints bought for him. And, if a person comes up in a pub and buys you a pint, you've got to take it. It's quite offensive to that person not to take the drink. Fame isn't what it's packaged to be.

TOM ROBINSON

I chose life

Or, making the leap to recovery

TR: If you have depression it's kind of like you have an alcohol problem: somebody who has been an alcoholic is never not an alcoholic; somebody who has been a depressive never stops being a depressive. What you can say is, 'I'm a depressive in recovery.' I've been on an even keel for ten years but I can't say I've beaten it.

SP: *You said at an early age you had these dark thoughts and these troubles and you attempted suicide. What pulled you back from the brink and, from there on, what gave you that direction of going, 'No, life is* *worth living, and not only is it worth living, I'm going to have an impact on others in this manner.'*

TR: An incredible chance was offered to me. It doesn't exist today, it didn't exist for most people then, but this opening occurred in that dark despair. I was seeing psychiatrists, I was being sent to mental hospital, I was really looking to find another way to top myself, when I was offered an interview at a place called Finchden Manor, and my dad picked me up from boarding school and drove me down to this place.

We drove right to the heart of Kent, near Rye, and turned into this courtyard on the outskirts of a village where there was this Jacobean manor house, half ruined. All the windows had been smashed and broken, then re-mended, and then smashed and mended again. You know, loads of times over forty years. And there was a row of ragged faces looking out of the window as we pulled up in the courtyard. We got out and went to the front door and were ushered into this calm, oak-panelled place. A door opened and we were ushered in and this little, stooping man with sort of black, plastic glasses, which were quite dirty, came toward us in an old tweed jacket, and he took my hand in both of his and peered into my eyes. He held on to my hand for too long; he didn't let go, so he made sure I was engaged. And then he looked me in the eye and he went, 'You're very lonely, aren't you?' And, all these psychiatrists I'd been going to, saying, 'This is an ink blot test, tell us what you see in here...' or, 'You're going to take these pills at this time...' And this man just looked straight in my soul.

I could've cried on the spot because that was the heart of what was wrong: it's not 'you're homosexual' or 'you're depressed', it's 'you're lonely as fuck' and there I was. And he talked to me for about an hour, just me and him in his study, and just took this burden off my shoulders completely; just somebody who reached in, understood, communicated. He was born in the Victorian times; I mean, he was already gone 70, he was 75 or something at that time. But he'd been running that place for 40 years, and it was a therapeutic community for disturbed adolescents but run on the most unconventional lines imaginable. It wasn't regulated, it wasn't government sponsored, it was basically his private house in which our status was as guests staying with him and his wife. So, technically that was it, although he had a staff of ten.

In this old manor house, and its outbuildings and its grounds, which had a football field and ponds, and rose gardens, outbuildings, stables, everything, there were about 45 youths aged between about 14 and 25, and they were that old because they were never sent away because you'd reached a statutory age, if you weren't ready to leave. So, there was about 45 inhabitants, there were about 10 staff, 8 dogs, about 30 cats, and his one little section of the house, beautifully kept, absolutely civilized. The rest of it was just mayhem; the smell was indescribable. The boys did all the chores, did the cooking, cleaned the lavatories, all the rest of it. We just took it in turns on a chores list.

I was shown around after I'd seen him and he went and talked to my dad. And in my dad's diary he noted down that day, 'After one hour with George Lyward, the boy was transformed.' I went around the place and it was terrifying because these were boys who'd come from the most troubled backgrounds, you know. Some from borstal, some from mental hospital, some just like me from school, but all with quite deeply-troubled pasts and yet there was this kind of electric, alive atmosphere.

I was shown in at mealtime and we were all sat at trestle tables. Some had ragged jeans, in those days having hair down to your nipples was unheard of, and everyone shouting and sitting, and then boys bringing in the food, and others going, 'Seconds!' and all the food cooked by them. It couldn't have been more different from the Quaker boarding school where I'd just come from. And, at the end of the day, after I'd seen this alarming but vigorous environment, I went back to Mr Lyward and he said to me, 'Well, we're full up and we've got a long waiting list, we haven't got any room, can't take you. We don't normally take boys as sick as you.' And then he just turned to me and looked me in the eyes and said, 'Do you want to come?' And I went, 'YES!' He was seeing if I was ready to take the risk of jumping rather than wanting set conditions. If I was capable of making that leap, he would offer me that lifeline and I just leapt. And that's the best decision I ever made in my life: I chose life, rather than slow death back at home.

SP: *At that time, so much of mental illness was so misunderstood, so you would've been sent to so many different people who didn't know what they were doing, or didn't know how to diagnose these things. So what a personal and individual thing to experience, and add to that* *the beauty of that sudden accessibility to a community of like-minded people. Which, love or hate the Internet and social media, for all its negativity, it has opened up that accessibility to find other people. So, in the almost inevitable loneliness that everyone encounters at some point of teenage life, you can find other people that are feeling the same, that have been through the same, that have those emotions.*

I think one of the toughest things of depression can be a feeling of not having the right to be depressed, to be unhappy, to be miserable. As you were saying, there were so many people there who had come from tougher backgrounds and upbringings, and it can at points feel like, yeah, I've not got a right to be struggling, to be unhappy, because there are so many people in worse situations. There are, but that doesn't make your own struggles wrong, or any less important; it's still a valid place to be and feeling to have I guess.

TR: Totally, and that was the nature of the therapy; it was effectively group therapy, you lived in that community. And that is the thing about being part of a community: we're all connected, we're all part of one another and if I do something it's not in isolation, it affects all of us.

6

RACE

n the last few years race has been one of the most debated and challenging topics in society, and it's very much a subject that, I feel, should be being addressed by all of us, not just those negatively affected by it.

People like Killer Mike and Akala, and many others, were a joy to have on the podcast as they spoke so openly and astutely about all the issues surrounding race, and are always happy to engage in a debate on it with anyone, regardless of their race or heritage.

The thing that has seemed to anger me as much as anything this year has been those misunderstanding and speaking against the hashtag #BlackLivesMatter. This became a huge thing and a massive movement in the wake of numerous unequivocal injustices against the black communities in the US. People started to argue that the hashtag should be #AllLivesMatter, and that completely missed the point, because OF COURSE all lives matter. That's a given. And it SHOULD be a given that black lives matter, but, at this particular point in history (not to mention all of the other points in the past), that didn't appear to be the case.

I've heard the argument explained in many different ways and the simplest was along these lines: if you are at dinner with your family and everyone is given food except you then you will be angered by this. If you are told you don't get any food today then you may respond by saying that you deserve to eat. You would be right. If your parents were to respond with 'EVERYONE deserves to eat' then, while that would obviously be true, it really wouldn't help the situation at hand.

And that, very basically, is why the black lives matter hashtag remains so genuinely important. It is NOT an anti-white people movement; it is a pro-equality movement. You wanting to eat when excluded – as in the above scenario – is not anti anyone else eating, it's simply wanting to get to the same level so that all of you can eat together.

Race came up many times in the different episodes of the podcast and it is, of course, always a somewhat nervous area for a white guy from Essex to know how and where he may engage in such debate. But I have been lucky enough to have amazing guests that DON'T have their guard up and AREN'T on the attack, which really is the epitome of that and many other movements going on right now.

Honest discussion, without threat or judgement, is one of the essential cogs in moving this debate forward.

KILLER MIKE

A human problem

Or, without hope, anything is up for grabs

SP: *With everything going on in Ferguson, your voice feels like a very important one at the moment – I guess partly because of the Run The Jewels stuff, perhaps – but it feels like you have the ear of the black community and the white community. And I feel like the problems going on at the moment need attention from both sides. It's not just something the black community can heal, and it's not something that just the white community can heal.*

KM: It's a human problem. As humans we have allowed ourselves to get comfortable in boxes we were put into. We've allowed ourselves to be cordoned off like animals. We've allowed ourselves to be separated by sex, by religion, race, by creed, by colour, when at the end of the day we're only human beings. You're white, with long hair and a narrow nose, because at some point humans migrated out of Africa to a colder climate, so their noses needed to be narrower, their hair needed to be longer to keep their face warm. And recessive genes reduced the pigmentation. That's pretty much the only difference. We're still both human beings, you know? Civilization started on the continent of Africa so we are as much the same with our small differences.

With that said, no human being should live under the tyranny of government if promised freedom. And America prides itself on the story we're told from the time we're five years up – that we broke free from the tyranny of taxation and monarchy. There was a little riot called the Boston Tea Party that we celebrate. My people, black people in America, are only 51 years into that promise of freedom, because we had to fight: we won ourselves out of slavery, got our full rights, after the Alabama period all that was wiped away, then we got back into a series of Jim Crow, then we had to fight for our civil rights again, which won not only *our* civil rights, but won civil rights for more people than us. We had no civil rights, and for the last 51 years, we've just been B-level citizens. And I'm tired of being a B-level citizen. I was promised everything the United States preamble, Bill of Rights and Constitution gave me, and that's what I want. And I don't want that just for me, I want that for my neighbours who may not agree with my lifestyle; I want that for people who don't agree with me period, because we deserve that based on, 'This is what this country promises us.' And even if a country has not promised that, I am a human being and I have inalienable rights that were given to me – that are God-given. To live as long as I want to live; to live peacefully and not hurt others; to procreate and live and die peacefully. I shouldn't have to be a battery for a war machine. I shouldn't have to try to figure things out outside of the realm of my real possibility. So for me, it's important for me not only to speak as a black person – because I know I'm black and I have a responsibility as a black man to speak and say, 'Hey, you're looking at unemployment as 8 per cent but excuse me, Mr President, it's at 14 per cent for me.' I have that responsibility.

But bigger than that, I have to come to the same conclusion that Martin King came to after he earned civil rights on behalf of melanated people; what he discovered was, the same conditions that are creating the oppression that suppresses this group of black people in America, they suppress white people in the appellations that are poor; they suppress the Asians that were used to build the railroads system; they suppress the Native Americans whose land was stolen to put on reserves. And he started to understand that this really is a thing of poverty; that it really is a perpetual war machine. It really is the tyranny of government and their different ways. And that's when his focus shifted. So for me to just keep arguing the black side doesn't take the fight where it really belongs. The fight really is a human fight against a system.

SP: *I think it might be a slightly different fight, for example, if the police were armed over here. Because I think over here the poverty line isn't as heavily weighted in race. Over here there's a lot of white people who would end up having the same things done to them. And then I think it wouldn't be as easy for the media to push it as just a race thing.*

KM: So it's important that I speak to both sides and both people. You're white, and we share some of the same experiences, so I have empathy, and I definitely have sympathy for people who have suffered enough. There is a special set of BS that black people go through in America. There's a whole other set of rules for us. And with that said, we have a responsibility to organize on our behalf, but to also be voices and advocates for people globally that are treated like us. In some countries where there are no black people, there's a whole other group of white people that for whatever reason get oppressed. And we ought to be examples of what can potentially come good out of that. How can you organize, plot, plan and strategize and mobilize your way out of it? I'm down for advocates and allies no matter what your race, creed or colour.

SP: *It's a huge question, but what do you think the solution is? Or a path in that right direction? I went to one of the rallies over here for Michael Brown and it was a strange experience for me because I felt like I needed to be there to show my respects, but equally I felt, what is this doing? And I argued with people a bit because it sounds like I'm saying the only solution is violence, but to me, standing there and protesting in the way that a system prefers you to protest, when what you're protesting is that system seems somewhat redundant to me. It's not just the police that's the issue here, it's the people who've cleared the police. So – particularly in England where it's all cleared and sanctioned – we've had permission to come and protest at this point. But it's the system that you've had permission from; the system that you're protesting against. So again, I left feeling, I'm glad I went but I felt it needed more. It needs something else.*

KM: Part of it is ceremony: you need the ceremony because people need to experience camaraderie. You have these beliefs, I have these beliefs; you and I live thousands of miles from one another, but at a protest and a rally you get to see the camaraderie. For a black kid who's getting the shit kicked out of them by the cops three or four times a year, that shit is going to be very lonely. 'Why the fuck is this just happening to me?' But when you turn up to a rally, sanctioned or not, and see people who look like *you*, I understand I have allies that look like the people that I perceive as being my oppressors. And if I understand that from a human level it doesn't allow that grain of hatred to grow past the system. So what remains is the hatred of the system and the upholders of the system. So you need the ceremony – sanctioned and unsanctioned. You need these ceremonies because they allow people the opportunity to congregate and it allows people the ability to see. And it shows governments and institutions the number of sympathisers that come after that.

SP: *I think it shows the government and the system that, but equally it shows, with protests in different states, it shows that it's not just a Ferguson thing; and equally in England, in Europe, that it's a human problem. It's not a Ferguson problem.*

KM: Some of the most touching things I've seen are pictures from Palestinian children that say 'Black Lives Matter', or 'We Understand'. Syrian children. You get to see children in parts of Africa. It just matters because, man, it sure doesn't feel as lonely. It sure doesn't feel as lonely. And a lot of times that hopelessness is what will have a child strapping a bomb to their chest. If you wipe out the ability to hope, anything is up for grabs. But if you leave the ability to see that there are people advocating for you, even if you don't see them on a daily basis – there are people that care about your campaign – then you maintain hope, so that you don't have to go to the extreme of violence. And the other thing is, if the system does not change by the will of the people then it is the responsibility of the people to attack and take down tyrants, by whatever means necessary.

KILLER MIKE, cont'd

White privilege and the police

Or, I need you for an ally

SP: *Something I've seen a lot of white people getting confused about is the term 'white privilege'. I'm seeing a lot of people who are working class saying, 'I've not got white privilege; I'm working class.' But I think it needs to be explained how much of a misconception people have of the term 'white privilege'. It's not about getting all the breaks.*

KM: Yeah. You have the benefit of doubt that isn't afforded to others. It's not saying, 'You're bad, you have white privilege.' No, you have the benefit of doubt. There are certain things – when a white mother puts a coat on a child, it's 'Go outside, come back in, don't talk to strangers.' The stranger is the danger. When a black child goes outside – 20 years ago and today – it's, 'Go outside, do not talk to strangers, do not get in the way of policemen...' It turns into a whole grocery list of things that no child should have to think about. A child should only have to think about 'Do I have on my coat? Do I have on my mittens and hat?' That's it. That simple. But black children don't have that, not in America. Especially our boys; our boys have to learn by the time they're 12 and 13. Forget kidnappers and killers and gang members, and all the other fear things that are thrown at you through television; you have to worry about the police, and the people your parents pay tax to sanctioning their child's murder. And that's just a different set of worries.

So white privilege isn't about saying, 'Oh, you've got it better than me, we hate you.' No, it's just saying, 'You get a break. And since you do, I need you for an ally. Because you understand what it means to work hard – you're a tradesman, you get it too, but I need you for an ally over here.' The police chief in Richmond, California, which can be a very violent place – a very wild place for black and brown people in particular – stood up with a sign yesterday saying 'Black Lives Matter'.

That is pretty weighty, that is pretty heavy, because he is breaking ranks with policemen nationally. He isn't castigating police, he isn't saying, 'I don't believe you,' he is simply saying, 'The lives of the people I police matter.' Think about that. There is a policeman saying, 'The lives of the people I police matter.' And if more policemen had that attitude you would see more cops thinking before a trigger is pulled. I think the police need more of that.

SP: *It just blows my mind that that is a statement that needs to be made. It is a hugely big deal, but when you strip it down, that should be a given. That shouldn't have to be made. But at this point it does.*

KM: Police don't get out of their cars any more because there's only one. There should be two police in a car. Police should be required to get out of their cars for a number of hours and walk and meet people.

SP: *My grandad was a policeman and I'm proud of that, because he was a good policeman. He was one of the good guys. It's not to say that there aren't any of them any more, but you don't get to see if they are or are not because they're behind a screen.*

KM: And our police are becoming more like special forces.

SP: *But they're not training them like special forces. And that's a huge concern from this side of the pond, seeing that we do have armed police over here but they are trained – they know what they're doing. So some defence of some of the stuff that's been going on in America, you know, 'Someone has panicked...' That's not a defence. That should not be an option. And again, it comes back to white privilege: if the excuse comes back to 'Someone panicked' – they wouldn't have panicked in the same way if that was a white face that was there. There would have been a more controlled approach.*

KM: There was a white protester early on in Ferguson that said, 'At 18 years old I shot a policeman with a BB gun and I am still alive.' Think of the power of that statement. I was reading a passage by Noam Chomsky today that said Reagan was a vehement racist – and this is Noam Chomsky saying this, this isn't a black rapper that's saying this. He said he was a vehement racist and he used a war on drugs to criminalize just being a black man. And eventually that pours over into other ethnic groups. We have had a cold race war going on against black men in my country since they landed there. And we didn't come voluntarily. Someone came and got us. But there has been this fear, this paranoia since then. If Nat Turner moments were going to happen they would have happened again and again by now. Black people are just trying to be regular citizens, enjoy a good life, live a regular life and die happy, the same as everyone else. But it feels like we're being cast in a part of a play that we didn't volunteer to be a part of. I don't want to be your goon, I don't want to be the bad guy in your story. Tell your story. Go find a real bad guy. I just want to live and exist. We have the same human conditions that everyone else has. When people say black on black crime – what do you mean? Black on black crime? Black on black crime happens because you have crime among the people who live near each other. If you live in an all-white community, burglaries aren't called white on white crime, they're just called burglaries. So you get burglaries, you get murder, you get that in any community, but for the State to use that as an excuse to sanction murder? No.

SP: *Let's go back to some solutions. There was a song three years ago now, I think, by B Dolan and Sage Francis called 'Film the Police'. It felt like something that has been painfully relevant, repeatedly over the years. But something I've felt has been a backlash in what I've observed online is people saying how filming the police isn't going to help because of the clear video footage in the Eric Garner case.*

KM: This is what's going to happen: either these cops are going to start being held accountable, and you're going to start seeing prosecutions happen and cops that are abusing power going to jail so other cops are going to have to adjust their behaviour; or you're going to start seeing people attacking policemen in the street. That's it. There's no way around it. Those are the two alternatives. And if you don't believe me, there was just a black and a white cop arresting a guy in Baltimore; they were a bit too rough with the guy – a white guy walked up to the cop and snuffed him. You know, tried to knock him out. In New York, some of those Times Square cops were in the middle just looking crazy trying to arrest someone, and someone threw a barrier at the cop and hit him. People are frustrated. Everybody has been lied to by a cop. Everybody has had a speeding ticket lie or jaywalking. Everyone has enough distrust that it is believable. And when a system becomes that, the proletariat is going to push back. Repression breeds rebellion every day. If you didn't study civics or world history you skipped over this thing called the French Revolution – if only one set of people seem to have it good, then the people on the bottom are eventually going to rise up.

SP: *History plays a huge part in it. In the UK I think we are terrible at protest, at action in change. France is amazing at it. I remember reading a while back when they were trying to bring in wheel clamps; clamping cars that were parked illegally. The French as one put glue in the clamps. So instantly the authorities had to stop doing it, because they rose up. But England, our history is going out as one and conquering. There's no history of going against; we've always been a part of it. Whereas the French have more of a civil revolution element to their history. So what do you think the choices are there in America. Is it an inevitability? The dismissal of filming the police is, I think, misplaced, because the reason we're seeing everything now is because of people filming the police. There's not been a sudden crazy increase of police malpractice, it's just being caught on camera, and being brought into the public eye. Therefore, as much as it's fucking horrific to see video evidence of someone being choked to death ignored, it's being seen and it's being addressed and causing the noise that we're hearing now. I feel it's wrongly dismissed in that way because even if the prosecution isn't there, it will end up sadly being the catalyst to another solution.*

KM: It needs to be filmed. Because if you do get to the point where you're burning police stations down, you need to be able to pull up YouTube and say, 'These are the reasons. This is the reason for this.'

SP: *The other thing I've witnessed a lot of is the backlash of people defending the police. It's something I've argued with a lot. I keep referencing B Dolan but he's speaking a lot online about this. In one of his posts he said, 'If you're watching this video and your first reaction is to defend the police, then you're in the wrong place in your mind.' I get where* *people are coming from because, again, with the whole filming the police thing – I don't think all police are evil or bad – but that isn't the issue at the moment. The issue that's being discussed is the ones that are, the ones that are doing terrible shit and getting away with it. It feels it needs to be clarified to them: it's not saying 'fuck the police' as such, it's saying 'fuck the crooked police'. Fuck any police that may not be crooked but are riding with and not taking any action against crooked police.*

KM: Yeah, common sense seems to be something that a lot of cops leave in their lockers. I watched a video once; there was a kid walking by a protest. He wasn't in the protest. It might have been a protest for Palestine or the Muslim community. He was just a black kid walking by. Security guards or police come up to him, grab him, he's like, 'I don't even understand what's going on.' Then they made him. All that time, people are walking with him and the cops saying, 'He is not the right guy. He didn't do anything.' And the cop is just so dead set on his instincts being right that it caused that kid to suffer.

If you look at Eric Garner, at the time the cops were trying to arrest him, people were telling them: 'He didn't do anything.' And at some point, if you're a beat cop, beat cops who used to walk the block would have had enough sense to say, 'Hold on. Let me figure out what's going on.' Because it's stupid to arrest someone and say 'let the courts figure it out' when you are the first line of offence and defence and you could have solved that problem. And if you don't have the common sense to solve that problem there, you don't have the common sense to be policing. And if your answer to dealing with someone whose one hand is already under control by three other cops, a man you already have in a prone position because he's on his side, and his other hand is out saying, 'I can't breathe,' is to keep an illegal chokehold on him? My gut instinct says, I wish someone would have walked by with a .38 and put a bullet in your head and kept walking. That is my gut instinct. But going to my civil instincts, my civil instincts say, you should not be a cop. Because your ego and your narcissistic instinct to say 'you didn't listen to what I told you' overcame your ability to preserve human life and get to a proper understanding. I'm like you: I pray that the protest and the civil way works, because the alternative is rarely easy. There are always more of you than there are cops; there are always more of you than there are of government; the proletariat is always bigger than the rulers, and at any given time, those give and takes could swing the other way. And that is my thing. Do it now, and do it right while you can because when people get fed up, they're going to burn everything to the ground.

SP: *Something you touched on there of not being fit to be a cop is incredibly valid, because, again, it feels like there was a time when the cops were the great and the good. I used to work in a record store – there were people who applied for a job in the record store, didn't get a job and ended up joining the police force because they couldn't get a job in the record store. That doesn't feel like the kind of people we should have running the streets. Is there an answer to that? At the moment the police – rightfully so – are being vilified. So I can't see why anyone with a straight head would want to become a police officer. And that's a negative thing, surely? Surely it would be better if the police was full of people who were more reasoned. But at the moment, fuck, I wouldn't go near that uniform.*

KM: Two of my cousins are police officers, and they're good cops, and I respect them. A friend of mine, she's about to enter police academy. Right now. And she's going to make a great cop, because she's fair.

SP: *That is the solution. That's a long-term thing, but surely one of the long-term solutions is to get good people from all communities policing.*

KM: Yes, you need people from THE community policing – even if you can't police in your direct neighbourhood because that's a direct conflict of interests, we need policemen who are from where the communities are from. We need people who understand the working class, who understand poverty, we need people to understand racism in a certain way. We don't need someone who just got back from Iraq, couldn't find a job and is now being told to police regular citizens the same way they policed in war. It's not right. You need to have people who understand the psychology of the neighbourhoods they're policing. That means as a cop you should be seen at the PTA meetings, you should be seen at the corner store, and you should be seen on your patrol. Not just on your patrol, because when you ride through on your patrol, you're just an outsider that comes through. You're perceived as someone who's just there to pick somebody up. You aren't seen as a saviour, you aren't seen as an ally because you don't ever get out of the car.

SP: *You aren't a person, you are just a cop. Which is the vilified thing right now. What do you see as the key progressions and changes at this point that regular individuals should make? Do you think just more things like that that the regular person can do to take responsibility for themselves and their community?*

KM: Yes, you have to do, locally, what you can do: vote locally, think locally, act locally, buy locally. Ferguson is 70 per cent black. Think about that: 70 per cent. Like the mother of that child said, 'I lived here my whole life.' Darren Wilson moved here. She has more rights to be in that community and to determine what goes on. But if you are in the community you have to be active. Your police chief or sergeant should know you. You should have a community board and push for a community advisory board or community liaison board for your police departments. 'How do I make that happen?' You vote for an alder-man, you vote for a councilman, *make* them do it. Or vote their ass out. Demand that your policemen – my wife told me that, you can call the police, you can have the police come to your child's school – the policemen that police your community should have to introduce them-selves to the parents at the PTA meeting. Parents should take their ass to the PTA meetings. The only way these problems are going to get solved is if they are solved at a local level and they grow nationally. Our Constitution and our republic is made in a way so that federal govern-ment can't just shoot mandates down to stay their local laws because that disrupts the sovereignty of states, but it can go the other way. But it has to remain a grassroots movement. And on the local level you have to become so active that you cannot be ignored. And that changes the fabric of the way things work. I truly believe that. With me it's going to be either/or. We're going to work it in the way the system allows us to because we're a free republic that's based on voting, that's a democratic republic. Or we're going to do what our forefathers did and burn it to the ground and start over. Those are the only two ways. There is no other way. Either you get it right in the way the system has allowed for us to do it right, and that means the system and allies within the system have to comply, or we burn it to the ground and start again.

SP: *That's why the crazy bloody-mindedness of the system has got to break, surely. Because the best solution for everyone is the first solution rather than it have to be a public uprising if, on a global scale, it grows more and more likely.*

KM: Yes, because people are tired of fighting wars and they don't know why they're fighting. People don't even know why they hate each other any more. I don't even know why police hate black men any more. It ain't like we're out there shooting at the police, which we could be. You could sit there at the store and someone could lay on the top of a roof, take an AR-15 and put a bullet through your head. It ain't that hard. But the fact that that isn't happening in the community shows you this community ain't no hyper-violent community. It's a community without jobs. And you as a policeman should be advocating to bring jobs back to your community because that makes your job easier. Because then you are just patrolling the TV factory making sure no one's stolen a TV; you aren't worrying about 30 kids out on the block trying to find excitement.

RIZ AHMED

Limiting our stories

Or, heads in the sand

RA: It's interesting, the differences in the UK and the US TV and film industries. One thing I've seen is just the amount of roles out there if you're not white. I think it's just a little bit of a tragic waste what happens here. I think we can't just think that our best days as a country are behind us, that our best stories are behind us. Our best stories were when everyone wore a bonnet and ran around the countryside. Surely not, man?

The UK still is a cultural powerhouse, partly because of the Empire and partly because of multiculturalism. Look at our contemporary musical output. Every couple of years kids in London invent a new musical genre that takes over the world. Literature-wise, our multiculturalism spawned everyone from— in modern art, you've got Christopher Ofili, Tracey Emin talks about her mixed heritage. Literature you've got Zadie Smith. I just feel contemporary British reality is on the coalface of multiculturalism and we're really advanced in how we're dealing with it – when you look at continental Europe. We've got such a global story to tell over here and I feel like a lot of the time we retreat into this very tried and tested package of days gone by, which actually I don't think is as exciting as our contemporary stories.

And it's weird. I've been out there in America doing this HBO thing and who pops up to play one of my co-stars? It's Bashy. And you get that kind of stuff happening all the time. If you're not white and you are an actor in Britain, the opportunities are – it's embarrassing. I've found a lot of my work has been coming from the States for the past three or four years, since I did *The Reluctant Fundamentalist* with Mira Nair. And then I did the pilot for *Criminal Justice* and *Nightcrawler,* and now I'm back doing the series for *Criminal Justice.* And already being out there I've got three American offers lined up for every one British one. And it's a strange thing.

SP: *Why do you think the British industry is going in that direction? Obviously they've taken a lot of money out of funding, but why can't people see that modern Britain has a lot of stories to tell?*

RA: I think it's a symptom of a wider societal squeeze that's going on right now. If you don't have money, you've basically been shafted in the last few years: students have to pay more to go to university, or if you're on disability benefits... The amount of people who can afford to have their lives subsidized to go and work for free in the creative industries and be apprentices – whether it's at *Vogue* or making tea on a film set – it's just more and more of the elite in our society. Which is white middle and upper class. So that's why it starts skewing the stories that get told. And I think it's also post-financial crash – people want to take less risks so they fall back on tried-and-tested formulas: period drama is something that's always worked in this country and it's sold globally; *Downton Abbey* absolutely smashed it. It's also, during times of crisis, they say escapism sells. And that means harking back to bygone days when things were simpler, which is part of it – rather than facing our fucked-up, contemporary reality. So I think it's a lot of head-in-the-sand stuff mixed with less resources stuff, which leads to this really weird skew. People like Lenny Henry have been really vocal about this as well, and there have been loads of campaigns happening because black and ethnic minority representation on TV went down for the first time in ages. If we carry on sleeping on it we're going to become this irrelevant pastiche; this artefact, as opposed to what we are in other creative mediums, whether it's visual art or literature or music, which is vibrant and contemporary.

SP: *It puts a limit on everything, because there isn't a limit to stories of Britain, but there is a limit to Elizabethan stories in Britain. That time was only a set period, so if all we're going to stick with is that sort of thing, then we're going to run out of ideas. Before you broke into acting you got a degree in philosophy, politics and economics, and then went into acting. What made you go from that path to an acting path? Obviously you were studying something so away from acting, what made or influenced that switch?*

RA: I was always acting at school and at uni, but I've always been quite a restless person. I couldn't see myself in a desk job. Another thing I was doing a lot of at uni was music, running these club nights. I started this club night called Hit 'n' Run, which still runs in Manchester under Rich Reason. And that was drum 'n' bass and hip-hop. And that was my passion, along with acting. But I thought I could never really have a career in it. I remember so specifically this girl at university that I didn't even know that well but was an acquaintance, and I just remember she randomly emailed me and she said, 'I saw you in this play you did a couple of months ago and you'd better be pursuing that, because you should.'

And it was so weird. No one had ever said 'you could make a career out of this'. All I needed was one little nudge, because I doubted it so much. Partly because turning on the TV there was *Goodness Gracious Me* and that was it for a long time, growing up. Though I think what those guys did was incredible and amazing – actually, Sanjeev Bhaskar's a childhood hero. Anyway, this wonderful girl gave me this nudge and I thought, yeah, maybe I should. Screw it.

So yeah, it was a very personal little moment of random good vibes. If you can randomly give people good vibes, you should do it, because it might affect their life.

AKALA

The myth of a homogenous nation
Or, people have been migrating forever

SP: *There is a general feeling we're seeing around the world now that 'immigrants are bad', 'immigration's bad'. It's quite crazy when you think every country – literally every country – is built on immigration. So you're saying immigration from* now *is bad?*

A: We're in Kensington and Chelsea: we're in the wealthiest borough in Britain right now, which also has a lot of poverty in it as well. There's a whole bunch of Islamic immigrants just south of this borough who are billionaires. But that's not who we're talking about when we say immigration. This is what I mean when I talk about race and class. When we talk about Muslim migrations here, who have we got an issue with? It's not billionaires from oil-rich Gulf states who buy Ferraris and McLarens and keep all the hotels in Kensington and Knightsbridge full: we haven't got a problem with them. So even though they're the 'wrong' religion, even though they're the 'wrong' race, their money and their allegiance to the British elite means they're not a problem. They're not the immigrants we mean: it's the poor people. Even though many of those rich people can be proven to be allied to certain ideologies and to be funding certain ideologies, it doesn't matter if they keep the money flowing and keep putting the money into certain people's back pockets.

SP: *The scariest part for me is that the immigrants that the majority of the UK who are against immigration is talking about are fictional immigrants: they're immigrants that aren't real people. They're these versions of them you've read about, and heard these fear-mongering stories about, so it's crazy that there's such uproar over a fictional thing. It comes back to greater education.*

A: It comes down to greater education.

SP: *Or providing of information. It's both the things we've talked about: education, and free and more open and accurate media. Rather than, 'We can say what we want; we can rescind some of it down the line but that's not going to be paid any attention to.'*

A: I think the sad thing is, whether we like it or not, the mainstream isn't going anywhere, and people aren't going to turn off those channels. So I think – as people involved in alternative media – we have to create our own platforms and, where possible, interact with and engage with putting different information on those popular platforms. All of the uproar around immigration this year and during the election is really about distracting us from the problems of this society. The ruling elite in this society, like the ruling elite in most societies, have displayed immense corruption: they're giving £700 billion to their mates who ruin the economy, privatizing everything from here to kingdom come, creating all sorts of problems within society that are totally unnecessary. Britain is a very wealthy society; it has more than enough money to feed, clothe, house, educate and provide healthcare for every person in this country, many times over.

SP: *That has to be made clear when people respond to immigration with things like, 'Well, once we've sorted out our own homeless issues then we can think about the rest of the world as well.' No, those are things that are in the budget and cash flow of the country.*

A: (a) The problem isn't with people coming here, and (b) most of the people who've come here are skilled, qualified. We've got to make up our minds – if we don't like immigrants, we shouldn't use the NHS, because immigrants built it. Make up your mind. I'm fine with it: if you don't like immigrants, die, instead of letting the Bangladeshi woman or the Ghanaian woman save you.

SP: *There's a Doug Stanhope bit where he's saying about how, in America, the nearer to Mexico you get the more there are people saying, 'There's people coming over: they can't speak the language, they can't do basic things,' and yet they also say, 'They're stealing our jobs.' If you're losing your job to someone who can't even speak the language, you're pretty crap at your job. If in your mind the people coming over here are such a drain on society, and they're stealing your job, then you need to up your fucking game. You can't have both of those two fictions in play at the same time.*

A: They can't be useless, lazy, welfare-claimants and also taking your jobs. If you're going to go with a stereotype, at least be consistent. The hypocrisy with Britain is the amount of British people living abroad. It runs well into the millions. The history of this country is of founding settler colonial states in South Africa, in Kenya, in Zimbabwe, in America – all of those descendants still live there. When I was over in Zimbabwe, there were over a million people of British descent who still live there, most of whom are quite wealthy, despite what people want to tell you. All of whom live very well, despite how people want to portray it, which is why they haven't come back. So we've got to make up our minds. We can't act like this kind of small, victimized, tiny little island when this country was once a huge global empire. Make up your mind.

Britain had 52 countries that it claimed to be the mother of; mother country of the British Commonwealth, and the vast majority of people who have immigrated into this country are from the British Commonwealth. We've got to make up our mind: if we are willing to muster the military might of the British armed forces to save the Syrian people – because we love them, apparently – yet we don't want them in our country, there's a contradiction there. So if the truth is there's some British strategic interest to protect there, don't insult the British public. Say, look, it's an oil region, or we're against Iran, whatever it is, whatever the strategic interest is, just be honest with the British public. Which isn't going to happen; but it's not because we love Syrians, otherwise we'd be welcoming them into the country.

Incidentally, a lot of people like to forget this today: during Nazi Germany, Britain also refused to take a lot of Jewish people, and described them – particularly in the *Daily Mail* – in remarkably similar ways to the way we're describing people coming from Syria today. Today, because there is a genuine respect for the Holocaust as a particularly horrid event, no one wants to look back and admit Britain refused to take a lot of those migrants. But that's what happened. And so I feel the British elite has learned nothing. Most ordinary people are decent people, I believe. The way you can tell that is, if you look where UKIP [UK Independence Party] received all their votes, it is where there are no immigrants. The people who don't know any immigrants are the ones who hate immigrants. It's an inverse map: it's an inverse to where the populations of immigration are high and where UKIP got their votes.

SP: *It's fascinating because – not to be unnecessarily goading or disrespectful to UKIP supporters – that fact just tells you that generally they are that bit further in the past. In areas where in the seventies and eighties African families came to South London, where Asian families came into the Midlands, all over the country, they're not the areas that have this issue because they've got to know this; they've seen this, they've built, they've grown. Whereas now that's spread out – it's taken ten, twenty, thirty years – now that's starting to happen, they're starting to have those fears that Londoners had – and it turned out alright. It turned out OK. It turned out to be a healthy society.*

A: I'm not going to pretend London is a paradise, because it isn't, but for all its faults, in many ways it is a model – and quite a remarkable model. Not because of the British elite, I'd say in spite of them. Particularly in working-class London. I grew up in Archway, Holloway, around there. My neighbourhood had kids from Somalia, India, Cyprus, Ireland, Turkey, Jamaica, Ghana, working-class white English; we even had a lot of middle- and upper-class kids. Race was there. In primary school it didn't matter so much, in secondary school we did become stratified by race because of experience. All the young black boys started hanging around together because of the way teachers stereotyped us, and because getting searched by the police and other experiences socialize you into groups, but we still all kind of interacted and the main tension was not race. Black boys were not fighting Asian boys. In fact, the Asian boys were fighting each other, the black boys were fighting each other and the white boys were fighting each other. It was almost like the violence was segregated into groups. There was some cross-cultural violence but most of it was not based around race. So it's a really interesting new culture.

If you look at young people in London today – again, I'm not saying it's a utopia, but it's a remarkable degree more than probably any other place on the planet – there is such a diverse range of people living next to each other in relative peace. That is quite fascinating about London as a model. And actually it makes me very proud. Even if I don't feel very British, or English, I feel very much like a Londoner. I feel very much that this city has shaped me and who I am, and I wouldn't have had the experiences I've had or the interactions I've had with Cypriot culture or Gujarati culture or Turkish people or Irish people anywhere else in the world. While still retaining the proudness of who I am and what I am. London is very unique and amazing. And it seems current policy is trying to destroy all that, pushing out all the poor people.

SP: *That's the irony: when we were this great empire, supposedly, we were going to all these places and saying how great Britain is. You're telling everyone how amazing Britain is but then a few years later going, 'No, it's not for you...'*

A: The funny thing is this mythology that Britain was once this homogenous place. When? Go back to the Industrial Revolution: even then, conditions for workers were so bad in London that every year they had to replenish the working population with immigrants; immigrants from Eastern Europe; immigrants from Ireland; immigrants from all over the world. Granted, many of those immigrants were 'European' and what today we'd call white. Nonetheless, immigration on the island has been a constant. And it's not just the case for Britain: there is a history of the movement of peoples around the world, which has been a constant ever since the Ethiopian *Australopithecus*, Dinknesh, which they call Lucy. To quote a friend of mine: people have been migrating forever.

AKALA, cont'd

The racialization of poverty

Or, we're happy to be multicultural for wealth

A: I read in the news the day before yesterday that the Conservatives have said they're building a prison in Jamaica – costing £25 million – to send back all of the Jamaican criminals to Jamaica. And because of all the scaremongering, even *I* thought there were more Jamaican criminals in UK prisons than there actually are. It's actually 700 people. And there are more Irish and more Polish in Britain's prisons than Jamaicans. There are over 10,000 foreign nationals in Britain's prisons. This is all according to the *Daily Mail*, so this is the most right-wing statistics available, and still they had to admit it.

Why aren't we sending back the Irish? Well, because we've got a special relationship with them. Why aren't we sending back the Polish? Oh, because their prisons are already full. So I can't help but cynically think, is this the first step towards sending back British-born people of Jamaican origin? Because what else could be the motivation for Britain to spend £25 million, in a recession, supposedly, on building a prison in a foreign British Commonwealth country?

So then I think of George Osborne saying he's going to get rid of free school meals. As someone who grew up on free school meals, I'm like, hold on a minute, what you're saying is you want people to starve. Because there are literally children in this country who, through no fault of their own, are born into families with no money who will not eat if there are no free school meals. How do you expect a child to learn if there are no free school meals? What you're saying is, you want this child to go on the street, because if I'm not eating breakfast and my only chance for a meal is at school, and school is no longer providing free meals and I'm hungry, and I'm 14, what am I going to do at that point? And the local drug dealer is saying, 'Yo fam, you can make £200 a day, all you've got to do is x, y and z.' If it's a choice between that and starving... Are they actually trying to turn poverty in this country back one hundred years?

SP: *It feels like it harks back to our obsession with American culture in many ways because America's had that for so long, of turning the ghettos into what they are. This was just an area where poor people lived but we'll demonize it and put enough restrictions on it that it is now an area where you don't want to go at night because there are drug dealers. In many situations not through choice, it's through the forcing of circumstance and situation on to people.*

A: I'll give you a specific example: Compton – probably the most famous ghetto in America – was a middle-class neighbourhood in the sixties. A lot of people don't know that. That's why it looks so nice. Originally it was a middle-class white neighbourhood, then a lot of the socially upward, mobile, black population started to move in and it became a black neighbourhood – still middle-class, because most of the black population in Compton worked at two huge car factories. Those car factories closed down: overnight Compton went from 80 per cent employment to 80 per cent unemployment. And that's when the gangs came in, that's when the poverty came in. So the people who were willing to work hard, who had nice middle-class lives, were in a stable neighbourhood, with no risk of violence…

SP: *It's circumstance – you can't put that down to anything intrinsic in their experience.*

A: Maybe now people are making choices – some people, to get out of the hood, however we want to cut it. The decision to outsource work to Asia because it was cheaper, because the bottom line made more profit, had very real consequences for poor neighbourhoods across the country and that was part of design policy.

In America poverty is so racialized. If you want to find a black neighbourhood in any American city, just look for where the freeway is. Because in the sixties, during a period called 'urban renewal' – also known as 'nigger removal' – they built motorways over all of the black neighbourhoods so people didn't have to drive through them, so no commerce would be created. The Bronx is like that, there's a freeway that comes from outside the suburbs into Manhattan. In Chicago it's like that. In LA it's like that. So you have these isolated islands that are an outcome of policy. France has the same. And it seems that England will not be satisfied – or at least certain factions of the British elite will not be satisfied – until we go from being one of the most multicultural, one of the most diverse, one of the most peaceful major cities of that kind of range of population or range of income and really culturally interesting, into an ethnically homogenous place; with a touch of Russian, Middle Eastern, African and Indian billionaires, of course – one can never get rid of those; we're happy to be multicultural for wealth.

SAUL WILLIAMS

Technology as witness

Or, the forced hand of transparency

SP: *Technology has come along and developed because of the exploitation of societies and countries that we, in the Western world, can go out and exploit. But it's getting to the point where technology is becoming that bit more affordable and global, and therefore potentially could be the gradual solution to things like that. We see countries with Twitter, where there's a new media, with blocks on the media – but it's now got to a point where people can talk to the world themselves.*

SW: Exactly, and that's the thing that balances the equation, and that's the thing that's interesting about modern technology. It's interesting to know, for example, that the continent of Africa is the continent with the largest number of people connected to the web, that it's the only continent where the majority of the population is under 25. You think of statistics like that and go, 'Oh, ok, that's the future.' You think of where these e-waste camps exist, where people are going and starting to strip these things and rebuild out of waste, and create satellites and 3D printers in places they can actually use these things. I read recently about someone being able to build a 3D printer near these mining camps in Sierra Leone where rebels had chopped off the hands and arms of miners in order to punish the foreign corporations who hired them to work for them.

SP: *Essentially sabotaging their tools: the tools just happened to be humans.*

SW: Exactly. So there are villages of amputees where people are building 3D printers out of found objects and all of a sudden are selling $20 or $30 prosthetic arms and hands that are robotic. And they work because they're 3D printed and we found a way to use the technology to serve us and not to place that high price tag on this thing that could be readily available for many.

SP: *It's a beautiful thing as it starts to slip through the hands of those who were originally trying to control the world with it, as it starts to get into the hands of regular people. That's the exciting thing.*

SW: The prosthetic robot hands of the regular people.

SP: *Exactly. They're ironically going to end up being able to have the Internet in their prosthetic robot arm...*
This might seem a bit of a jump, but 2014 and 2015 will I think stand out as being looked upon in America as some dark times for black America. Some real horrendous things are going on, but equally it's also the time where technology has allowed those stories to be told.

SW: That's what makes it the times that you're expressing: those things have been going on for as long as I've been alive and at the same exact rate, the entire time.

SP: *But now everyone's carrying a camera.*

SW: Everyone's carrying a camera. We know how and where to point them, and we have a means of sharing them; and that changes a lot – at least on the surface. And it allows us to spark and instigate greater and greater dialogue, and to force, perhaps, the rate of change at a quicker rate. So that's what's going on – it just brings us back to technology.

Because that is analogue: a policeman kicking some dude's ass dead in Baltimore, that's analogue murder. It's been going on for a long fucking time.

SP: *It's a tough one to try and engage and debate on online, particularly as a white male. Even though there are great tragedies and horrendous things going on; there are cases being thrown out of court that should have at least resulted in charges. But the fact is three or four years ago, that case would have happened and there wouldn't have been outrage about it. So it's certainly not at a corrective point yet but it's getting that attention, building that outrage, so we can start looking to move on.*

SW: I grew up going to the same protests; I grew up on the State Capitol steps with my parents, marching. The outrage was there. It's not the outrage that's new or that wouldn't be there, it's the other side: it's the judge now who has access to more than the prosecuting attorneys' ideas and can actually look for themselves and study some statistics and go, 'Holy crap, maybe these guys are right. Maybe there is some connection.' And also they're not allowed to hide the connections to the sheriff's office and all these things. So all of a sudden this forced hand of transparency is revealing the cracks in the system and the structural and systemic powers that are angled against social change; these guys are being revealed.

Oftentimes we stand on the shoulders of our ancestors and oftentimes we stand on their necks. And the problem is that there's also a lot of fucked-up shit in the system and in our systems. And we all have that circulating around us. Even when we self-identify as black, white, whatever – we start to use their slogans to define us. Only because we've agreed upon these terms and allowed ourselves to be slotted under this banner, which is, oftentimes, most times, all times, much less than what we are as humans, as beings of breath, and sound, and wind, and music, and change, and poetry, and art, and all these things of expression and creation. We are so much more than a fucking colour.

7

POLITICS, MEDIA AND THE LAW

firmly believe that the growth of podcasts in the last few years is largely down to the failings of the mainstream media. So, as an avid listener of podcasts as well as being a podcaster myself, I struggle to be that mad at the appalling level so much of the media has dragged itself down to.

As papers and news channels became more and more blatantly agenda driven, podcasts started to pop up as this free, uncontrolled alternative. Suddenly you had access to the uncensored thoughts and views of people from all walks of life – and it was free.

Two podcasts we chose not to include extracts from in this book were specials I did with two charities: the British Red Cross and Housing for Women. In each one I was put in touch with people who had been through unimaginable challenges, but wanted to share their story. Ramelle, a refugee from the Democratic Republic of Congo, and Mira, a young lady brought to this country for sex trafficking. Both of these conversations were incredibly hard to have, and equally hard to listen to, but they were true stories of real events.

At points they were graphic, but this was always at the wish of the guest, wanting not to shy away from the horrific things humans do to other humans. Even when the stories were told through tears it was with the belief that they MUST be heard and should no longer be ignored because of the discomfort we get when hearing them.

Both of these stories were an honor to be able to provide a platform for, but the thing that struck me as they went out and the overwhelming reactions started to come in was that these stories could NOT have been told in the main stream media.

They WOULD have been censored.

They WOULD have been edited.

But, in the podcast world, that isn't the case.

Podcasting provided a platform for both of these women to say, 'No. I shouldn't be made to feel ashamed of what I have been through.

I shouldn't have to hide away from the truth. I did nothing wrong in these situations. It is THEY, not I, who should be ashamed.'

What's more, podcasts can freely discuss politics and points of law with no pressure or bias. No forced agendas or lines to be towed.

I haven't had a single politician on the podcast, yet there has been SO much discussion of politics and legal process as these are things that affect so many of us. And there is always the space and time for open discussion and debate, regardless of the views that come up, as there are no 'powers that be' dictating the company line on particular subjects.

I firmly believe that as podcasts grow they will gradually see the death or at least the removal of power and control of the agenda-driven mainstream media.

BILLY BRAGG

Politics isn't just for politicians

Or, cynicism is our greatest enemy

BB: When people ask why I didn't go into politics, there's a really simple answer: politics is too important to be left to politicians. Why should I have to be a politician to talk about politics? This means life and death to me, so I can talk about what I want to talk about. I had to learn pretty sharp, and my education was the miners' strike, because I was going up to those gigs in the north of England. And the people who'd organized them – who were highly politically motivated, who were Marxists, who were Trotskyites, really political – they wanted to know what the fuck I was doing. Was I just some pop star from London who didn't know his shit? Or did I actually have half an idea about why I was doing this?

SP: *That's a great baptism of fire, right?*

BB: Yeah, it was, because you were sleeping on their sofas. So you'd end up round their house after a couple of beers, you'd be buzzed up from the gig, and then all of a sudden you're really...

SP: *It's* Question Time, *as such.*

BB: Yeah, it was good, it was good, because it put you on your toes. They have their own language the Marxists, they have a language they talk, and you kind of have to learn their language. And sadly for them that language doesn't mean shit to anybody any more, which is a problem, because the things that Marx talked about have not been resolved. So in some ways we've got to find a new language, a new way to talk about these things. But that's what poets are for, you know? That's their job, that's why we're here.

Russell Brand's stand on not voting was a bit of a shock trooper move: he wants to sort of use shock and awe arguments, so 'don't vote' is good for that.

SP: *It's an instant way of getting people's attention.*

BB: Yeah. And there are times when that makes sense; there are other times when it doesn't make sense. You know, 'don't vote' doesn't make sense when you're trying to get the BNP [British National Party] out of Barking. It doesn't make sense: it's a really bad tactic. And there are other times when maybe there's only a small handful of candidates and they are all very similar – and we have had some elections like that over the last few years – but I've still been motivated to get out there and bite their ankles because that's just the way I feel. Because it's not either/or. I mean, that's the argument I used to have with the SWP [Socialist Workers Party]. It's not, you know, 'If you'll come into the ballot box with me at election time, I'll come out on the streets with you at revolution time,' you know. It's not, 'I'm either a revolutionary or I'm a Labour party supporter.' It doesn't work like that.

SP: *That's a great point, I've never really heard it expressed that way.*

BB: Malcolm X said 'by any means necessary'. He didn't mean by shooting people. There's always a photograph of that quote where he's looking out a window with a shooter. He didn't mean that. He meant, whatever method you have to be able to take the bastards on, you should use it. That includes the ballot box, it includes the debate, it includes whatever means are proffered to you.

So for a young generation to have the opportunity to vote is important, and there are some really interesting opportunities with parties like the Greens. People see that there is an alternative to what they've traditionally voted for.

SP: *And I think – love or hate either of them – the rise of the Greens and UKIP, if nothing else, highlights the fact that you can no longer use the argument of 'they're all the same', because the Greens and UKIP aren't the same. You can't say that. You could have argued that with Labour and the Conservatives; even with the Lib Dems when they were starting to come through. But you can't argue that, so the excuse of not voting because they're all the same is just, 'Nah, sorry.'*

BB: I think a better argument than all the parties being the same – and I recognize why people feel that way – but I think a better argument is that they've all run out of ideas. I think that's a more fair argument, because I don't think they are all the same. I think Ed Miliband is probably the most left-wing Labour leader in the last 25 years and there's probably not another one there like him. But I think they're running out of ideas. They operate within very narrow parameters of what they think is possible, which is basically what the *Daily Mail* thinks is possible.

And the thing about the Greens and the SNP [Scottish National Party] is they're willing to break out of that stranglehold of centrism and offer something genuinely interesting, and you can see what's happening in Scotland, how the SNP are becoming more popular. If the Greens could build up support it would have the opportunity to start bringing people further towards more left-wing ideas. We need people to keep putting forward alternatives to austerity because it ain't really going to work: it's already been shown in Greece that since they've brought austerity in to make the economy grow, actually debt has grown. So the medicine ain't working.

There's also the fact that we're still living on cheap credit, and that's what got us into trouble last time, economically. The reason we're living on cheap credit is because Thatcher smashed the unions. And now there's no one in the workplace putting pressure on employers to do right by people and pay them a proper day's wage. And because there's not that pressure any more, all the money's gone off to shareholders and bosses, corporate bosses, and this has undermined the ability of consumers to live on their wages, so it's all cheap credit. And, ultimately, it's not going to take too long until we're going to be back where we were.

SP: *I remember a tweet you did, when Thatcher died, and I thought it summed things up really well, saying that celebrating the death of an old lady is fruitless because the damage she's done hasn't died; the damage that's been done to the nation hasn't died. So I'm not going to be sitting there going, 'Yeahhh, Thatcher's dead!' In a way it doesn't make any difference to me.*

BB: Yes, it's a reminder. What I said was her death is a reminder of how we ended up in the situation we find ourselves in, you know?

SP: *There's nothing to celebrate.*

BB: The death of an infirm little old lady is not going to change anything. If you really want to do something about it, then don't mourn: organize, get in there. Stop the cynicism – because that is our greatest enemy.

AKALA

It takes a certain type of human to want to be president

Or, politics is fucking complicated

A: Obama is a fantastic politician; I don't think he's a fantastic human. I look at his record on speaking about police brutality in America, which has been very obvious; I look at the fact he was willing to bomb an

African country; I look at the fact he continued most of Bush's wars... I judge the man on what he's done, not on what he said he'd do when he came in. And I didn't get happy just because his dad's black – I look at what actually happened. But he's an incredible politician: he's an incredibly intelligent man, he's charismatic.

SP: *Until a year or two I would have agreed with you. It felt like Obama came in with all these promises and ideas, then just fell into line like everyone else. It's only a theory, but it feels like, now, he spent his first term playing the game. The way both of our political systems are set up (unless you're a dictator overthrowing another dictator), it's almost impossible to come in and have huge change; it has to be a gradual thing. Again, it may be to an unforgivable extent, I'm not decided on it yet. It feels like Obama came in and appeased people who were against things he believed, but now it feels like he's in his final term they almost can't touch him now: he's making those moves with gay marriage, with the Confederate flag... And he has genuinely been one of the first to bring up the gun debate, the arms debate.*

It feels that where I spent the first four years going, 'Fuck this guy, he's not doing anything,' I now look at him and think it could be the case that he's played this game really well: spending a few years to back up his power. It's crazy to think the role of president of the United States of America isn't actually that powerful a position. There are a lot of people behind that, so it feels that maybe he's built his power up there by getting the right people onside, or moving people out, changing things around slightly. Now he's able to go, right, we're changing the gay marriage law. His speech after one of the recent spate of shootings blew me away because it didn't feel like a president making a statement. He stood there and said: 'This is the eighth time I have had to do this this year. At some point we're going to have to admit that we're not doing it right. At some point we're going to have to look at Australia, Portugal, and go, we're not doing it right.'

A: For me, I think that he's obviously an incredibly intelligent man, and for a man of his level of education to want to be the president of the United States of America, knowing everything that that entails; knowing that that obviously means overseeing murder; knowing that that entails deciding who lives and who dies; knowing that entails knowing certain amounts about the world and not revealing it to the public; knowing all the things that come with that office. I think that takes a certain type of human even to be able to do that. I'm not passing judgement on that. I've never been in that world: I wasn't educated at Harvard, I've never had the desire to lead a country in the current form countries are operated; I'm fairly sure that if I actually had to be the prime minster of Britain or the president of America, or even the leader of a revolutionary Pan-African nation, I'd still have to make some pretty shit decisions.

SP: *Obviously we're saying it takes a certain type of person to do that type of thing, but I think that can be a positive and a negative.*

A: I think, for Obama, he was never going to come in and be able to change America from a historically racist, classist, imperialist power.

SP: *He was also the first black president, so to come in and make huge changes then – it's so tough.*

A: But I don't know – and only he could answer this, because only he's in his own soul and his own head – I am very doubtful, to be honest with you, despite the rhetoric, that that was his genuine aim. I think he's centre-right. He's not Donald Trump, he's not Ben Carson, he's not even George Bush. He's not as crazy as all those people, fine. But he believes inherently in the justice of America, he believes in American exceptionalism, he believes to some degree, whether he realizes it or not, as an extension of that, in the superiority of white people.

What do I mean by that? America was founded on that assumption. If we believe America is so exceptional and so wonderful, there is that idea underpinning that a bit. He believes in America's right to police the world. So he's not in line with what I believe about how the world should run, or how the world should be. Does that mean he's an inherently evil, insane psychopath? No. Does that mean everything he's going to do is bad? No. He's tried to do Obamacare, he's, as you said, with gay marriage, around the fringes of things, there's been some room for manoeuvre that he's tried to leave a positive legacy. And people will judge him on that.

For me, what was unforgivable with Obama, just for me personally, is to continue the wars he's continued and then be the president that oversaw NATO's bombing of Libya. For me, there's something really symbolically weird about the first African-American president deciding to bomb an African country and support people who – we saw how they behaved – sodomized the head of state with a knife in public. They didn't put him on trial and give evidence and say, 'This is why we dislike the guy and this is why he's going to jail,' or even, 'This is why we're going to kill him.' They behaved in a very vicious, disgraceful manner; the weapons that they stole are part of what's causing the spread of terrorism across West Africa right now. They stole weapons from Gaddafi's cache, so the consequences of the invasion of Libya, apart from destroying that country and creating the migrant crisis, have let terrorism spread all across West Africa, wreaked all kind of havoc, and whatever he does in America, however nice his legacy may or may not be for American people, that foreign policy fuck up – if it was even that – for me, personally, is unforgivable.

And him being handsome and having a lovely wife and a great family and being half-Kenyan doesn't make that forgivable for me. If he was a white guy, ironically, we would see that symbolically as much worse. Bill Clinton did bomb Sudan – people loved him because he was charismatic and played saxophone – but I think it would be easier for black people to be more like, 'Hold on, that's an African country.' Alright, an Arab-speaking African country, so people may not feel as connected to it as they do to Ghana, but there's something that's very symbolic about that happening that doesn't feel right for me.

SP: *I completely understand. It's interesting how, again, you point out there that charisma and certain associations – the fact that he's of African descent – come into play. I was someone sitting there thinking, 'That's pretty cool,' when he came out and said his favourite ever TV character was Omar from* The Wire. *Dude's fucking cool!*

A: I get it! Charisma plays a huge role in our attraction to people and there is no doubting he is a very brilliant man. No one is doubting that he is very educated, charismatic, as I said, for a politician he's a good-looking, smooth, great speaker. I don't mean that in the patronizing way that people say 'he's a black guy and he speaks well', I mean full stop, on any level, for any group of people. He is a performer. He is mesmerising.

I would love to see someone of that range of talents put that range of talents to their community for justice, the way Martin Luther King did, the way that Malcolm X did. That isn't possible for Obama, and that's fine. But, for me, he won't go on the wall with those people because as president of America that just isn't possible. I think as president of most countries that's just not possible.

Even look at Mandela. For all the fantastic sacrifice that Mandela made in the struggle against apartheid, in his tenure as president of South Africa he had to make some pretty horrific decisions. He had to make the decision to maintain an economical apartheid but enable political apartheid decolonization because at that point he thought that was the best he could hope for. And the legacy of that has been what? An ANC government shooting dead 32 miners at Marikana in 2012. Striking miners. They could never get away with shooting 32 white people without international outcry. So you have this legacy where the same brutality is woven into the system. I am not laying that at Mandela's doorstep; what I'm saying is even the greatest humanitarian – who exuded so much charisma, confidence, brilliance, love, despite everything he'd been through – even for someone like him, running a country is a difficult thing. This is why I get less idealistic as I get older. Running a country is incredibly difficult.

I'll give one more example. If we take Toussaint Louverture; Toussaint was the leader of the Haitian revolution – the only successful slave revolution in the whole of humanity. And even he, when he had won the island from the French, he maintained a semi-slave economy, only this time, the enslaved people got wages. Because he felt that pragmatically it wasn't possible at that point to say, well, all these people (slave masters) have done all this awful stuff; let's just kick them off the island. He felt pragmatically, to run a country, he still needed those people. They had the qualifications; they could run the plantations, etc. So he said, 'Cool, you just have to pay the people now.' And obviously the enslaved people were like, what do you mean? We're not going to work for the same people who have been torturing us for hundreds of years. He had to try and balance all those forces, even as someone who had been enslaved himself. Because politics is fucking complicated.

SP: *Politics and, I think, the way we are as humans.*

RUFUS HOUND

The game is rigged

Or, the vampirism of the economic elite

RH: There has been a shift in the last 50 years of going from being a citizen to being a consumer, and your value is now being decided by your habits as a consumer; which are now broken down based on what you tweet, what you write down on Facebook, what you like, what friends you have, and what they like and where they're based. You are now numbers on a spreadsheet. Your personhood is eroded.

Essentially there is a tiny number of people who live as free men on this earth. I say free men and you as a right-minded liberal listening to this might go, 'Oh, you said "men", actually "men and women".' Actually, pretty much exclusively men; this game is largely being won by men. White men. Just 85 individuals have the same wealth in this country as the bottom 40 per cent. But at that kind of money you live genuinely free. We know that when you're incredibly wealthy the law doesn't really apply to you. You avoid your taxes when you're incredibly wealthy. You eventually go to HMRC and agree to pay, maybe, ten per cent of what you actually owe, and they'll negotiate with you and then that's what you're going to pay. If you're a scaffolder and don't pay your taxes you'll do six months inside.

SP: *There's no negotiation there.*

RH: No, no, you're off. So when you're incredibly rich the laws don't apply to you. Society doesn't really matter to you: you exist outside it all. The nature of modern capitalism to me means most people are scared of change, because that's just the standard evolved monkey response to everything. It starts with fear. So people are scared of what changing it might mean.

SP: *It's the thing that angers me the most about our blind following of democracy. Number one, there are a lot of options other than democracy, but number two, there are a lot of versions of democracy that aren't the paper-thin masquerade of democracy that we currently live under. But it's the same with capitalism.*

RH: The countries whose economic growth has been more stable do have different notions of investing back in social infrastructure. Germany, South Korea, Sweden – their economies all took a dip, but they do not have the bonus culture, the selling off of public housing, the non-building of new housing, the lack of investment in that infrastructure that we have in this country. It's fucking insanity what's going on here, and it's ideologically driven. You want to bail out the banks? Well, OK, but you've got to have a fucking watertight system whereby we're going to get that money back.

It's not the 99 per cent, it's the 99.99999999 per cent you know; it's such a tiny fraction of people who are just rinsing the rest of us. And the problem is that those are the people with the money. And once you've got the money you've got the power, and once you've got the power you've basically got the opportunity to call the shots. Bear in mind even if you get caught out, ain't shit gonna happen to you, as we've found out from phone hacking. Absolutely James Murdoch wrote those cheques: so hang on, you're telling me the head of a company wrote a cheque for half a million quid and never asked what for? Never went, 'Oh actually – just due diligence – it might actually be my job to find out where this money goes'?

SP: *And it's become an acceptable defence! Ignorance isn't a defence; it's not a legitimate defence, and it wouldn't be for a regular person either.*

RH: 'I put on a blindfold, and then somebody told me to hold something and jerk my arm backwards and forwards, and then you know I could hear this screaming, but I just didn't feel like it was really my place to question where that screaming was coming from.'

SP: *Is this murder or prostitution? I'm not sure which charge we're on here.*

RH: Depends on what you've got in your hand.

SP: *Exactly ...*

RH: In essence the model I have in my head is: in those old schlocky Hammer Horror movies, where there's a castle with vampires in, all the villagers know that that's where the vampires live. And many of them work in the castle, and they won't say shit to them, because, all right, maybe a dozen virgins go missing every year, but you know something, I've got a job, he's got a job, so we'll just take it on the chin. And then once a year the vampires throw a big party and suddenly 50 villagers go missing.

Well this is, like, every day is a big party, every day is just the fucking vampirism of the economic elite and the financial sector; too big to fail, can't touch us. It sucks the life, literally sucks the lifeblood, out of what is meant to be our society.

What they've done is they've funnelled the money up. There was a big global financial crash and all the people with loads of money went, 'Oh, shit, I just lost a load of cash. Better get some back!' And they got some back from us.

SP: *Let's get it off the poor people.*

RH: If you're an atheist, which I am, there's this idea that we're this insignificant ball, spinning round an insignificant star, in an insignificant part of an insignificant galaxy in what may even prove to be an insignificant universe: who decided that these people got to have it all their way? We're all here from the same process of random chance, but the game is rigged.

RUSSELL BRAND

Better than fucked

Or, it's time for an alternative system

RB: I think what we have now is a kind of brutality and tyranny that's comparable to a Neanderthal horde bludgeoning everyone else into submission with fists and clubs – although it's more subversive and less obvious. I don't know if it was the meek who inherited the earth, but the sneaky inherited the earth.

SP: *We are in a situation where they are the most powerful – whether that was the physical, like in the past, or simply through money – and an individual can't compete with them. As a people we can come together and compete with them, but on a one-to-one basis in terms of equality, it's the same as the biggest guy in the playground.*

RB: What needs to change is that each individual needs to change, yes, but we need to have different social structures. If you just took David Cameron out of that job and stuck me in that job, things would be more or less the same, because it's a system. I'm an egotistical person, I'm a selfish person, I'm a greedy person. If you put me in a system that celebrates and elevates those values, you'll access that part of me.

SP: *I absolutely agree. It's the current system that we have. A dictatorship is seen as evil and could never work, because when we think of a dictatorship we think of negative dictators. Say, for example, when Barack Obama was coming through – he seemed like an amazing person. If he had got in and got to be a dictator, I think he would have been able to do a lot more good than he has been able to do within the political system in America. There's a video of him before he was even in line to be president or even talk about it, speaking about the trade embargo with Cuba; that we need to end it, it's archaic, it's done, yet he becomes* *president and it has to be renewed every year. That's clearly something that if he could just do what he wanted, he would have changed that. If he had been a dictator… A dictatorship can work if we happen to get a really good dictator – a really nice and wonderful and good dictator rather than an evil, tyrannous, corrupt dictator.*

RB: I think I agree with you in principle, but a guiding idea that came about as a result of writing this book [*Revolution*] is that concentration of power equals bad, de-concentration of power equals good; the more you can spread power, the better it is. When we talk about changing the systems and changing the structures that dominate currently, I feel that the alternative we need to have is not just 'let's get better people to do the jobs they're doing now'. What we need is to have people in charge of their own lives. I moved closer and closer to anarchism the more I thought about it, and I never thought I'd get to that because I always believed in the idea of great people creating great culture. But now I think everybody has got to create great culture.

SP: *A version of democracy that is always closest to being taken on by the anarchists was the Athenian democracy, where there were variations of it over the years.*

RB: Do you mean the poster shop or that place in the old days? Handsome man holding a baby in black and white?

SP: *And a female tennis player scratching her bum.*

RB: Kitten in a shoe. These people are our new leaders: there's a kitten in a shoe, a man holding a baby and a woman scratching her arse. Brilliant.

SP: *Yeah. The essential thing there with an Athenian democracy is that all things that are brought up to be discussed aren't judged upon by the government: you elect, say, a 20- or 30-person jury of the public – that is changed each time, so therefore it can't be corrupted – who are to make the vote on it. There will be mistakes because there is human error; but you won't have that evil person to blame. Then next time it comes around, it'll be changed.*

RB: Actual democracy. Because we have democracy in name but not in practice. I like that. One of the things I think is important is that people in the position of leadership should have the attitude of servants: 'We serve the people.' That UKIP leader gave a bit of lip service to it – 'You are my bosses' – but that's not a promise he can deliver on, because the structures aren't in place for the people in power to be in service; for the police force to remember that they serve us, the public, rather than being the enforcers of this establishment.

SP: *The problem with our democracy is it's a democracy with no exit. And not to keep going back to dictatorships, I'm not suggesting we have a dictatorship—*

RB: You don't half talk about it a lot.

SP: *The fact is, a dictatorship has an exit. It's a brutal, bloody one often, because it's an overthrowing, but the democracy that we currently have, there's not a tick box saying, 'I want something other than our current system.' So how do we address that? Is it through activism, through upris-ing, through forcing that change?*

RB: I think by activism, disobedience and forcing it. You and me on our own, say we're not paying our taxes, we're not paying our mortgage and our credit card bills, we're not voting, we're not paying any tax: we're going to go to prison. If me, you and 20,000 other people do that, that's a movement. When the financial system collapses, they get bailed out – there's money for that. When there's an Ebola crisis in Africa, there's no money available for that. So is money available, or is money not available?

SP: *It always infuriates me when the talk of democracy – of the current democracy – is that it's our best option. It's not. It's currently our only option. It's what we have. So that doesn't mean it's our best option, it's the only option you're offering us. So the only alternative is forced change. We have to take it upon ourselves.*

RB: The reason I said that 'no voting' thing – I was surprised by the amount of agitation that it caused. And I think the reason it did is because once you start going, 'What's the point? It's bullshit!' People go, 'No it isn't! It's not bullshit, it's democracy! People died for democracy!' Well, what's the difference? What difference does it make? No one wants the NHS to be dismantled: the NHS is being dismantled. I bet no one where we're from wants the Thameside library to be closed, which you told me is happening. Who can we vote for then?

SP: *I think the reason you will have that backlash from the no-voting thing is because of the short-form nature of all interviews and soundbites now. Not voting will be part of the solution; I'm sure you weren't thinking at the time that that's the big solution: we stop voting and everything is fixed. It's part of the solution, it's part of a greater solution. Through being active, through going out. And whether it be protesting, or whether it be not supporting certain companies or buying certain things, it can all work together to make a change.*

RB: Yes. The reason I said 'don't vote' is because I believe in democracy and we don't have democracy. If I feel I don't want the NHS shut, I don't want that library shut, I don't want immigrants being vilified, I don't want people with illnesses vilified, I don't want people with disability having their funds cut – who do I vote for? There's no one saying, 'Right, what we've done is we've noticed that we don't tax wealth, so wealth needs to be taxed. We've noticed that companies that operate out of our country are registered offshore. We're not signing any more trade agreements that increase corporate power. And all of the money that we get from that, and plus the money we get from not spending money on unnecessary wars, we're going to spend on feeding and clothing and educating the poor people of this country. And giving them power back.'

But the structures can't do it. That's why I think: break down power, devolution. The reason I think Scottish people were excited by that referendum was because it felt like some real change was being offered. I think, why not? An independent Scotland, an independent Manchester, an independent Essex, an independent London. Independent everything. Break everything down so people participate in a society of referendum. A society of direct democracy. Being directly empowered to control your own system. But that does mean you have to pay the price. Because some people will vote for things like, 'We don't want no more mosques built.' Oh shit. So there's got to be a responsible media and a well-informed populace. But I think direct democracy and representative democracy is a sensible way to go.

SP: *I agree. It's an interesting thing my brother put on his Facebook account and got fury from all his friends: the traditional saying of 'if you don't vote, you've not got a right to complain'; his post was 'if you vote, you've not got a right to complain' – because you're engaging in the system. If you don't believe in the system, yet you're engaging in it, how can you complain? If you're not voting because you believe in democracy, you can say, 'Yeah, I didn't vote, but because it's shit and I'm fucking furious about it.' Whereas if you're saying, 'I believe in it, but it didn't go my way', then how can you complain?*

RB: What I noticed when I looked at that experiment for direct democracy in Switzerland is that people still voted the way a big right-of-centre party would have had them vote. This is not a new idea, this is Chomsky's idea: the manufacturing of consent. If people's heads are full of an idea:

'Immigrants are causing you problems. Now vote: shall we get rid of immigrants?'

'Yes.'

But if you're given the information that *bankers* are creating the problems in your society then people will vote in that direction.

SP: *And it's hugely ignorant to assume that you can bring in this new system and it will work instantly because the people that are voting in this new system have been brought up on the previous system and brainwashed in certain ways. You can't write off a thing like that. People would argue it doesn't work because they've voted this way. Well, we've tried democracy for hundreds of years, so you need to try anything new for hundreds of years to say it does work or doesn't work.*

RB: Of course, we're not competing with perfection. 'Don't fuck with our system, we've worked it all out'. The planet's fifty to a hundred years away from total meltdown, there's massive inequality. So we're competing with something that's fucked anyway. All we've got to be is better than fucked. And what I genuinely believe is for ordinary people life will improve under a different system where there is more direct democracy and greater control of corporate power. There's no doubt about that. And the people who run the media are the corporate power; the people who work in government are the corporate power. So there's no way of getting any purchase on that argument, until people come together.

DR SUZI GAGE

Check the facts

Or, it's better to be right than first

SP: *Let's talk about the media misrepresentation of science, in particular with relation to drugs. We've obviously had the case recently of that poor lad who died and the first media reports were that he'd been using laughing gas – nitrous oxide. And obviously a while back there was the Causeway Cannibal, who they claimed was on bath salts: even now I will hear people talk about that as, 'Well, there was a guy who was on legal highs who went off and did all that.'*

SG: Well, technically he was, because he had alcohol in his system. I think he had alcohol and cannabis in his system, but he was quite clearly having a psychotic episode. Yeah, so that case was a man in Florida, I think. And he was filmed – it was really quite horrific – basically biting someone's face. It was really horrible stuff. But it went all over the media that bath salts – I think it was MDPV – caused it. They sensationalized it. There was also a story here, in Scunthorpe I think it was, where some boys died and it was all over the papers that they'd taken mephedrone. It turned out they'd thought they were taking mephedrone, but they'd actually bought methadone. So, all of these reports happen in the media well before the toxicology reports come back. And when the toxicology reports come back, you don't very often see, 'Oh look, actually, it was this.'

SP: *And even if you do, it's not remembered. It's that horrific thing in our modern media that it's more important to be first than to be right. Again, the Causeway Cannibal is a prime example of that – that's all anyone's going to remember. With a thing like that, when you hear about it, it turns into just talking among your friends about it, rather than continuing to keep an eye on it, because it's something that's happened and been resolved; he's been caught, you've got that tiny nugget of information you need to have a huge conversation at the pub about it. That's the scary and dangerous part of it. And when these things are readdressed, it's the typical thing in the press of making it a small correction.*

SG: If even that: that rarely ever happens.

SP: *On cases like this it rarely happens because I guess the person who you've misrepresented either isn't there to defend themselves because they've died or because they've got bigger things to worry about than what a paper has said about them; they're going to prison or whatever else. What do you see as ways to readdress this?*

SG: There are really amazing guidelines for reporting about suicide that are beginning to be noticed in the media, in the way that articles written about suicide are so much better than they were a few years ago. And I think it's because of these guidelines. So perhaps drug charities need to come up with these guidelines, too, to help the press to be a little bit more cautious before they draw conclusions on very little data. And perhaps the police as well in terms of the press releases that they give; being really careful not to add to this hysteria about a substance.

SP: *The people who should be the most controlled and calm are the media. But it does seem to be this panic of, 'We need to discuss this – they've done this drug we've not heard of and it's done this.' They should be the ones going, 'Right, let's research this, let's look into it. Oh right, it's not a problem, it's not a worry, we can calm down and relax.' I'd say it has increased in recent years; I would guess that's in reaction to the Internet. The fact is that the media has to beat Twitter or whoever else is talking about it. So there's that urgency to just go, 'Right, we just need our headline and we need to go now.' Rather than, 'Is this a fact?'*

SG: I think that's definitely a problem, and also they have to say something: you can't have one news organization that doesn't report on it.

SP: *Imagine a news station or outlet that only released completely researched information. I mean, that shouldn't be a weird thing, but if there was one that was always saying, 'Come to us, we'll have all your news four days later.' And they made a point of, it's four days later because we need four days to check and make sure everything's in and the stats are right. Making a point of going, 'We're not going to be the first, but we're going to be the most accurate and the most considered.' It would be a wonderful thing.*

SG: Quite often the problem isn't necessarily the actual article. Sometimes the article is written really well but it's the headline that's put on it. I write online for the *Guardian* so I get all of the fun stats and I can see how many people have read my article. I can see the average time spent on the page and they give me an estimation of the average time it would take to read the whole article. It's quite depressing! I've learned to put everything in the first paragraph now because I'm guessing that's probably all most people read.

SP: *And again, that's only increasing because of the preview functions on Facebook posts: you'll get a headline, you'll get a bit of a paragraph and a lot of people won't read a lot past that. They'll report it or go off into a rant and a rave. It's trying to push the general public to question things even once, I guess; obviously we can't expect to do the five-point checks that should be rooted in journalism. Just question it once and try and look into it.*

SG: There are some brilliant science journalists, I should say. I got a British Science Association Media Fellowship a couple of years ago and I spent six weeks over the summer during my PhD working for the BBC and I did three weeks working for the BBC Radio Science unit, and then three weeks writing news articles about science for the BBC website. Blogging is easy in comparison. When I blog I want to be topical and quite often I'm responding to an article, so I need to do that fairly quickly, but the science journalists at the BBC were writing more than a couple of articles a day, and I just could not keep up to begin with, at all. Because I'm used to going really in-depth into a subject and taking a really long time to think about what I want to say and how I want to say it. But they *have* to write.

The problem is, how can you be well informed when there's loads of misinformation all over the place?

HOWARD MARKS

Drugs and the law

Or, it's a flawed mess

HOWARD MARKS

SP: *Do you feel we're coming closer to legalization in this country? In America it was gradually conditional and now, in a lot of states, anyone can get a pass or a licence.*

HM: But it's federal law, you see. As all money is federal money, they can walk in at any time and take the lot. Also if you register as a marijuana user, addict or whatever in any of the states that have OK'd it so far, then you lose all federal benefits, like federal housing.

SP: *I was not aware of that.*

HM: Very few people are. You don't even have the right to own a firearm, not that most heads want to own a firearm, but you lose that right. Also you can be sacked without any reason, no reason whatsoever other than that you're a registered marijuana addict.

SP: *It becomes almost a dummy legalization.*

HM: It is a dummy legalization.

SP: *To kind of trick people into being relaxed about it.*

HM: For example, you can go to Las Vegas, which is one of the few places where you are allowed to gamble and make money and take it back home. That's ok. It's so inconsistent. The state/federal dichotomy has existed for a long time. There are several bodies of law about it.

SP: *It's such a confusing mess really.*

HM: It's a mess.

SP: *Essentially the states have chosen illegal choices, federally. No one is intervening at the moment. It's bizarre that you can be at such a conflict within one country and within one legal system.*

HM: I suppose they do it with the death penalty, don't they? States have total autonomy as to whether they will kill people or not.

SP: *There's that much looseness in the law essentially that you can turn around and say, 'Well, it is legal here for these reasons.' It's bizarre.*

HM: Some laws are wrong, I just don't agree with them, and I had no problem breaking those laws. Absolutely no problem at all.

SP: *I went to Amsterdam with someone who had never done any drugs at all, because they are illegal. And then in Amsterdam, because it was legal, they took some drugs after all this time in their life and it occurred to me how strange that is that you're not in any way morally or personally against something, it's purely that someone tells you it's not OK that you don't do it. With different countries it's purely a legality and technicality thing rather than a moral objective, which is bizarre that we accept it.*

HM: It is flawed. Because it is decriminalized rather than legalized. Decriminalized actually ends up criminalizing the thing more, because the more you decriminalize the more people are inclined to try it, so the demand for it will increase. As the supply remains illegal, you're further criminalizing it by your policy of decriminalization. Which doesn't make any sort of sense.

SP: *Again it's putting all the guilt on your side as the trafficker rather* *than those consuming it. Even now if you get caught with some for personal consumption it's a world of difference between being caught with intent to sell. These people that you're saying it's OK to have personal consumption didn't all go and grow that themselves and then import it themselves a joint at a time. That's supply and demand essentially.*

HM: The Dutch have a name for it, 'gedongen' or something like that, which is: alright, it doesn't matter how you got it or whether you're an illegal immigrant or a lump of dope or whatever; you're here, we'll deal with it as it is. If it gets there, it doesn't matter how it gets there. And Portugal similarly, they decriminalized simply because they thought it was a waste of money. They couldn't enforce it. They just gave up, really. And of course now they represent it as an extremely liberal society, but it was just the old bill giving up because they had no fucking money to do it. I cannot think of one rational explanation for prohibition. I just don't see it.

JON RONSON

The caped arm of the law

Or, why we can never have real superheroes

JR: About three years ago I was in Seattle with Phoenix Jones, who goes out every night to try and thwart crime. Costumed. With bulletproof vest and mask. He's been unmasked now, but he hadn't when I was with him.

Unless you count thousands of people screaming at you on Twitter as dangerous, that was the last dangerous thing that I did. Before I knew it we were surrounded by 30 armed crack dealers saying, 'If you don't get off our block, we're going to shoot you.' And I thought, I'm going to retire from doing really dangerous things because that was fucking terrifying.

His real name is Ben Fodor, but nobody knew that at the time. The problem with Phoenix was that, unlike the cops, unlike some cops, he got really frustrated when there wasn't any crime to thwart. He was a little too in love with thwarting crime. And when I was with him, there was very little crime to thwart. We saw these two men walking and one dropped something on the ground and Phoenix went, 'Yahtzee!' and went running towards them, thinking it was a drug deal, and said 'What did you drop there, sir?' And the guy said, 'Some pretzels.' So he was really frustrated that it was just a pretzel and not crack.

We broke up a gang of crack addicts at a bus stop. These sad, tired people at a bus stop. Phoenix and some of his fellow superheroes were standing whispering to each other, a distance off, and the crack addicts were looking at them thinking, what are these guys saying to each other? And do you know what they were actually saying to each other? One said to the other, 'I LOVE your colour scheme. I love the black and gold.' And the other guy said, 'Thank you very much. I had it specially made by a costumier.' 'Well, they've done a really good job. The gold really pops.' Someone actually said those words: 'The gold really pops.'

SP: *This is why we can never have real superheroes: it's never going to be for the right reasons.*

JR: Exactly. So then the crack addicts scattered, and that made me feel terrible. It was four in the morning, there was no one around, I just felt, leave them the fuck alone. I just felt it was hassling them, interfering with their lives. Like dogs chasing a fox. But then what happened was that on the last night Phoenix was so frustrated that I hadn't seen any real action that he decided to take me to Belltown. I didn't know anything about Belltown; I'm not from Seattle. This was a big story for them in *GQ*, it went viral.

We go to Belltown at three in the morning and there are about thirty crack dealers. I thought, we broke up a gang of crack addicts, that wasn't scary; we'll break up a gang of crack dealers, that won't be scary. I forgot that crack addicts and crack dealers are from two very different worlds. We got to Belltown and there were 30 people surrounding us saying, 'What the fuck are you doing here coming into our community in your stupid costumes?' And then one of them said to Phoenix, 'How you feed your family is not how we feed our family. This may be fun and games to you but it's not fun and games to us.'

So what I was doing, of course, was nodding in agreement with everything the crack dealers were saying in the hope that if the shooting started, they'd considerately shoot around me. And then they said – their specific words were – 'If you stay on our block we'll show you what the burner do.'

So, I am sure I remember from *The Wire* that a burner is a stolen mobile phone, but that doesn't sound contextually right. Then they walk away and I say to Phoenix, 'What's a burner?' And Phoenix says, 'That's a gun.' Then one of them comes round and walks past us. I can't remember his exact words but he basically said, 'If you don't leave our block now we're going to kill you.' Then he just circled round and goes back to the group.

Phoenix was like, 'Are we staying or are we leaving?' to his fellow superheroes. They were like, 'We're staying.' To make things even worse there was a parked car with a cigarette packet under the windscreen wiper. And Phoenix said, 'That is a sign that crack is sold here. So what I am going to do is rip this cigarette packet up.' And that's what he did. So then they all started walking towards us, about 15 to 20 people, and they had their hands down their sweatpants, and as they got to us they said to Phoenix, 'Are you really willing to die for this shit?' And Phoenix said, 'Yes I am, sir.' And they said, 'If you're really willing to die for this I guess we're going to have to go home. We should shoot you, but we're going to go home.' Then they all left.

SP: *What reasonable and controlled crack dealers. I'd imagine you just wanted to put your hand up and say, 'Excuse me, I'm not willing to die for this, so I'll just dive over here.'*

JR: It was an amazing thing to witness. Really frightening at the time. Phoenix said, 'We're going to stay around here to consolidate the block. Do you want to hang around with us?' I said, 'NO, I DO NOT!'

8

MISCELLANEOUS

f I'm honest, THIS is probably the category under which I should have logged the *Distraction Pieces* podcast in the first place. The beauty of the variety of guests and the openness of discussion on this podcast is that you really don't know what subjects will come up and, indeed, which ones will turn out to be truly fascinating.

One of the biggest reactions we have had over the whole run was to a bearded comic book writer discussing magic. Now tell me that could come anywhere other than under the heading of 'Miscellaneous'?!

As I have mentioned before, the idea of the podcast isn't just to have famous people on and hear their celebrity stories. The first and last criteria for guests is that they are someone I think would be interesting to talk to.

So whether it's Carla Valentine of Barts Pathology Museum discussing the relationship of and taboos around both sex and death, Paul Vickery of London's Prince Charles Cinema discussing independent cinema, Dr Suzi Gage discussing drug research or Jason Reed discussing international drug laws, there truly is nothing more important than it being an interesting discussion.

It has pleased me immensely over the year or two we have been running that, despite having some HUGE stars on the podcast, they haven't always been the ones that have generated the most interest and discussion. Without fail, regardless of pulling power, word spreads best when there is something of interest being said. Here's a selection of some of the most intriguing miscellaneous topics that have come up on *Distraction Pieces* over the last few years.

ALAN MOORE

What I talk about when I talk about magic

Or, putting the lights on

SP: *You discuss magic a lot, but from a belief point of view, a religious point of view almost – or philosophical.*

AM: I'm very, very serious about magic. Other than sports, which I assume was the hunters showing off, every other part of human culture evolves out of magic. Performance does; originally it's some guy probably dressed in a weird animal outfit, dancing in the flickering firelight making some sort of rhythmic sound. It's the shaman, originally. Written language and all representational art; these are such major steps forward in consciousness that the first person to actually employ them would have been in a shamanic context. And politics… Although it would have been an alpha male having that function in those early tribes, he would have had an advisor, who would probably have been the medicine man. So this is where it all started out.

One of the things we're arguing in the *Book of Magic* is that the entirety of our culture is pretty much the dismembered body of magic that we have taken apart, bit by bit. All that it has left today is, pretty much, empty theatrics. Now, that is not the way that I see magic. I see magic as the act of interacting with our own consciousness. Along with Julian James, I believe that before we understood what our consciousness was, we wouldn't have known that the voices in our heads were us; we wouldn't have a concept of mind; we wouldn't have a concept of dreams. The most logical way to interpret all of these things was a magical or shamanic world view. And that was not necessarily wrong, it was simply talking about a different level of experience.

Science is the most beautiful and elegant tool we have ever created for examining the material world around us. However, science cannot examine our consciousness because our consciousness is made up of things that are not repeatable in laboratory conditions. Science can map the areas of neural response in our brains when we're doing a certain thing, but that of course tells us nothing about the processes of thought. They're two different worlds. I believe that there is the material world and there is the world of our ideas. And I'd say that we tend to think of the material world as the real world. No, they're both real: our thoughts are real, they just aren't material.

SP: *Thoughts aren't a physical thing but they're everything. They're our everything. Our interpretation of everything isn't physical.*

AM: We do not experience reality directly. We only experience reality in our retinas, in the timpani of our ears, in the cilia of our nostrils. We experience our *perception* of reality. That's all we ever can experience.

SP: *Even the things we can physically see are our interpretation of it.*

AM: That world of ideas is the only world we will ever know. And so, whereas science is perfect for dealing with all of the things of the material world, we need something else to talk about what is to us the only real world – which is the immaterial world. And if you think about it, the material world is entirely founded upon that world of ideas. We have a physical chair, but that came from the idea of a chair. If we took away all the physical chairs in the world it wouldn't really matter that much as long as we still have the idea of the chair: then we'd know how to make it.

So the entire material world is standing upon this world of ideas and concepts and art. I believe that consciousness actually emerges at the same time as art and language. And I believe that this phenomenon is what you would call magic. That they are all synonymous with magic: consciousness is magic; art is magic; writing is magic. Especially writing. If you look at all of the magic gods, they're all the gods of language: Hermes, Mercury, Odin; all of them. Thoth – the Egyptian magic god – is also the scribe god. That's because language and words, yes, our entire reality inside our heads is made of words. We do not have consciousness until we have language. That doesn't sound right, I know, but that is what most language theorists accept. That language precedes consciousness. You don't have a concept of a thing until you've got a word for it.

So when I'm talking about magic, I'm talking about a more strenuous approach to your own consciousness, and when I say magic is art, I think there is a tendency for people to think, oh, right, so when he's talking about magic he's actually only talking about art. No. When I am talking about art, I am talking about magic. That is very different. I am talking about magic with all of the power and the astonishing range of effects you ever heard it had and I'm talking about that being possible through art. All of the things that magic claims to do – yes, it can do that, but only inside your head. Which is the only place it needs to happen. That is the answer to all of the questions such as, can I make myself fly? No, of course I can't because there's a law of gravity that flies against that. Can I project myself into an imaginary space where I am flying? Can I perhaps do that so forcefully that it will be a different state of consciousness where I will be receiving useful information of some sort? Yeah, I can do that.

It's not necessarily easy doing magic but it's quite possible and it's quite rational, once you accept this split between the material world and the immaterial world, and once you remember that they're both real.

SP: *That's fascinating. For a good few years now I've been working on a story I've never quite finished, but it lends to this perfectly. It's all about a guy who becomes comfortable with the difference between our waking reality and our dream reality. And it goes round in circles a bit, but in reality, the only difference between the two is waking up. If in your dream you become scared, your body reacts; if you're having an enjoyable time, you physically react. So how does the dream world come into your beliefs on reality then? Because surely that's completely in your head and therefore there are no limitations and no boundaries?*

AM: When I first became interested in what I thought of as magic, I thought it would make sense to look at what some other people had done and I thought it would be good to look at some of the systems that other people have come up with for understanding and mapping that territory. I found the Kabbalah – and I'm not talking about the Beckhams or Madonna. I'm talking about an original knowledge system that probably dates from round about the first century AD, some time around then, in Alexandria. And with that, you've got the sphere of dreams and the imagination. And you've got the material world – they're separate spheres. They're connected, but they're separate spheres. Now, in terms of how dreams fit in with all of this, I'd say— Are you familiar with the phenomena of lucid dreams? Have you had one?

SP: *I've got a friend who for many years had lucid dreams regularly. People say the most boring thing is when you tell someone about your dreams, but it became an obsession of his, because he had such control and such reality within them.*

AM: I think I've done it once or twice and it was extraordinary. Because you are entering this world of the unconscious, but you are entering it consciously. In normal dreams we are unconscious in the world of the unconscious: we do not know that we are dreaming. In a lucid dream, you suddenly wake up within the dream and are aware that it is a dream and thus become aware that you can control it, that it is all a product of you and that is it malleable, it can be shaped by your will.

SP: *The times I've ever come close to that, the times I've ever had any awareness that I'm in a dream, that's when I've snapped out of it and woken up. So I guess it's being able to take in that information...*

AM: ...and also to sustain that state, which is difficult and takes some practice. There seems to be some sensor mechanism in the brain that tries to trick you out of it. But it's very rewarding if you can get through that.

The way I see that fitting in is that if you can wake up in your dream and realize this is a dream, then you can take control of the dream. I think that is true of our normal waking life. That to a certain degree, all of us are living in a sleep. We are bombarded by the culture around us, we are lulled into a kind of complacent, waking dream. Realizing yourself – whether you want to call that magic or whatever you want to call it – realizing yourself as a person, as an individual, as an identity: that is like waking up. And you realize that, yeah, actually this very solid world around us, that's a dream too. That all started out in somebody's mind. This is all a more viscous dream.

In a lucid dream you decide that when you turn that corner there's going to be a brilliant mansion there and it's all going to be yours. In a lucid dream, yeah, you can do that – you can turn the corner and there will be your beautiful mansion. That can be done in the physical world as well; it just takes a lot longer. But the two worlds are very, very similar and when you wake up in them, then you can have a certain agency, you can actually effect and you can impose your own will, your own self, upon the dream stuff around you. Which is surely what every human being should have the chance to do.

SP: *If undistracted, more would hopefully have that as their wish.*

AM: This is the aim surely of all responsible art, and is the aim of all responsible magic. It's all about illumination. It's all about putting the lights on and seeing where we are. Trying to dispel some of this miasma of nonsense and irrelevance that we're surrounded by and actually see what our situation is. Putting the lights on. Magic, art, all those things: that's what they're for.

CARLA VALENTINE

Death out in the open

Or, it isn't morbid to think about death

SP: *Did you always have a curiosity with death or human remains?*

CV: It's one of those really difficult questions to answer, because I always inevitably get asked it, but I actually just always wanted to be a mortician. I did a lot of forensic research, I loved biology, I read a lot of Agatha Christie, so my main aim was to get into post-mortem work or autopsies. So I was quite single-minded from the age of about eight or nine, much to the horror of my mum, probably. We didn't have anyone in the family who was an undertaker or even a doctor, so she always says she has no idea where I heard about it – I probably watched *Quincy* or something like that and it just stuck with me.

SP: *It should be one of the most human curiosities to wonder about. I write a lot about death – it's something we generally shy away from and go 'that's sad' and move on, or be very blunt, rather than going into any great detail on it. It remains for most people an unexplored area. So I completely understand how from an early age you'd go, 'What is that? Why has no one explained this?' Particularly with children, with death you do actively under-explain: 'They're just gone now.'*

CV: 'The dog's gone to the farm.'

SP: *Yes, 'You carefully explain why I shouldn't go outside or talk to this person or do that, whereas this, you're being quite evasive.' So surely that ignited that interest more for you?*

CV: I think it did. If I did ask any questions I'm sure my mum had none of the answers. And there's nothing more frustrating as a kid, asking, 'Mum, why is this happening? And why has that happened?' and they reply, 'Oh, just because.' I started to read really early, at about two, so I think I was just getting hold of books. I remember going to the library at about ten or eleven and getting out A-level biology text books and the librarian just looking at me and saying, 'Shouldn't you be reading Enid Blyton and things like that?' And of course every child will have some brush with mortality, whether a pet dies— For me it was my grandad and, yeah, I had questions: 'What happened? Why did he look like that?' And no one would answer them for me, and that was around seven, eight years of age.

SP: *I think that's a really important thing and can be a wonderful thing, because children often won't have the programming that we have when we're older so there will be a more genuine curiosity of not knowing the questions you're not meant to ask. Because, in reality, why are you not meant to ask them? If you're wondering that, there should be that openness to discuss.*

CV: It should just be part of education. Children are innocently curious. When they see maggots or something, they're not being morbid, they're just genuinely wondering. You grow up and you get called morbid for wondering these things, but it's not really.

SP: *My mum used to be distraught when my nan, before any holiday, would tell her where everything was in case she died. My mum was always like, 'Just go and have a nice holiday – don't be thinking you're going to die.' She'd be like, 'Here's the books, here's the paperwork.' But again I was like, 'That's good, that's fine – she might die, you never know!'*

CV: It's just practical, isn't it? And also she was so ahead of her time because now there is this huge movement for people saying: you have to talk about death, you have to talk about what you want if you die. Ask your family if you want, have a death café, have a 'Death Over Dinner' event. There are all these things now happening as people are realizing that maybe shoving it under the carpet isn't the best option.

SP: *How do you feel we could go about making death not seem morbid? I got the morbid tag a lot because on my first album I had two songs about suicide and there was a song on the next one about domestic violence that eventually caused death. It was news to me that that was anything unusual: 'Hang on, I've taken something that's interesting in news and put it into pop culture and I didn't realize that was a confusing thing.' Death is something that definitely happens constantly – whereas it seems it was only the injection of it into pop culture that made it unusual or morbid or strange.*

CV: It is strange: we've had poetry and art that dealt so much with death – the Pre-Raphaelites, for example. It's odd that there is this sense of it being morbid when it is just life and what happens. Over the last few years there is definitely a death-positive movement. I knew a girl in the US termed it 'death-positive' because previously when we talked about things being out in the open it used to be sex. People used not to talk about sex so there was this 'sex-positive' movement, and they've kind of gone with that same template and tried to bring it out in the open. So at the moment you can do things like go to death cafés where people discuss aspects of death; there's Death Over Dinner, which is another thing in the US. And for me, I think when you're talking about death and the acceptance of it, there are two different strains as to why it's important. The first thing is a very practical strain: if we don't talk about death we don't want to think about it. When somebody close to us dies, we're not equipped to make arrangements, we're open to being taken advantage of by people who are in that industry, say, funeral directors. We're afraid of things because we don't know enough about them, like autopsies.

SP: *So being scared to discuss – you'll just nod and go with whatever they say rather than saying, 'What is this option?'*

CV: Yes, and people are getting on to that at the moment. Not to say that all funeral directors work in the same way at all, I'm not saying that. But there are certainly some who are taking advantage of that ignorance and that desire to get it all over and done with. So on a practical level that is going to cause issues.

The other strand to this issue is on a more mental level. There are a lot of studies that have been done over the last few years that say that thinking about your own mortality can really benefit you and make you really appreciate your life. It's nothing new. The Buddhists have been carrying out the 'nine cemetery contemplations' since the thirteenth century. They have this *maranasati* [meditation practice] where they think about decomposing corpses, the maggots, then dry remains, how they go into the earth... And it just makes them accept the level of life. There's nothing new or weird about thinking about death, it just seems to be a case of getting that message out there at the moment.

SP: *Completely. And I think the awareness of it, as you said, allows you to appreciate your life more or put everything in more perspective and not to be scared of it just because of the inevitability of it. It will always be mysterious, because there are different religions, different beliefs, but still, we do know that we are all going to face it at some point so it's ridiculous to have such a taboo around it.*

CV: It is, and I think also what's kind of ridiculous is this sense of moving away from what is natural. It's so much easier for people to accept this idea of embalming a corpse, for example – pumping them full of chemicals, which are damaging to the environment – and yet they won't accept being eaten by maggots and becoming maybe a rose bush or whatever. The more natural cycle of life seems unacceptable.

It's not that long ago that cremation appeared from nowhere and people were saying, 'It's awful, it's inhuman, it'll never catch on.' And now it's one of the most popular ways of disposal. Now we talk about alkaline hydrolysis, which is basically a kind of water blasting. They call it water cremation and people say, 'Oh no, it's disgusting, you can't turn people into sludge, it'll never catch on.' But the likelihood is it probably will within about 20 years or so. People will realize that it's not viable to keep doing what we're doing. That's why these discussions are important.

BLINDBOY

The art of outrage

Or, I predict a riot

BB: The Tate Gallery: that's what's called art today. There was a time when Manet would do a painting and it would cause a riot. Art doesn't cause riots any more.

SP: *It certainly doesn't.*

BB: Art in the Tate is nice to look at if you're part of a privileged, educated club. But what we call art today does not affect and touch the lives of ordinary people any more. So our whole thing is that what *does* affect people's lives is entertainment and the internet, so let's bring the ethos and thinking behind art and confront people with it through fucking entertainment, through songs, through melodies, through all of this. You're dancing and you're entertained, but you might walk away thinking of something existential: that's the purpose of art.

SP: *And it's kind of great as well because it feels like it can never be grabbed or stolen by the museums and galleries in the way that, say, Banksy's work has.*

BB: Tracey Emin's 'My Bed': I loved that. She did it inside a gallery but it made the front pages of the *Sun*. It outraged the person on the street: whether you liked or you didn't like it, it affected normal people. That's good art. But art galleries have turned into churches. A person will walk into an art gallery— You walk into the Tate and it's a big white space and most people in there are quite silent. And I believe the reason they're silent is because it's a very middle-class educated thing. They're terrified the person next to them will find out that they don't understand what that art on the wall is about. Because that is the big crime within art: 'I don't get it.'

SP: *I've been to a few exhibitions recently with my older brother who picks some really great stuff; he's really knowledgeable. And I walk round them in silence and will be excited to get out and say to him in private, 'I thought that was shit, I thought that was amazing,' but I wouldn't want to say it in there in case anyone else in there heard it.*

BB: It's like taking a Communion wafer and spitting it out in the priest's hand: it's sacrilege within that culture.

The other thing about high art is that the reason things are expensive within art, the reason things are worth millions, is not because they're brilliant, but that when art started to become very expensive, around the time of the Industrial Revolution, wealth tended to be handed down through generations. If your parents were wealthy, you were born wealthy. The Industrial Revolution allowed the emergence of what we now call the middle class. People who had been the working class through hard work started to own factories, so this new wealth came about. The people who were formerly at the top now had the same amount of wealth as the people who owned factories, but the people who owned factories were not educated. So if everybody can buy the Ferrari – we'll say as an example – the only thing you can't buy is taste, education and culture. And that's why art is expensive. If ten lads around you have got Ferraris and Bugattis, you can go, 'I've got a

Picasso and not only do I have a Picasso, I understand why it's good.' And that's why art's expensive. It's fucking horseshit. It is the egotistical masturbation of very, very rich people.

DANNY WALLACE

Charity guilt-tripping

Or, I'm not *not* trying to save a life

SP: *I've got a lot of weird views on charity in general and the fact that so much of it is you paying for a service: you're buying the right to feel like a nice person.*

DW: Yes, of course.

SP: *And it's fine, and I understand that, but I think it's grown hugely in recent years where there's pressure to do charity stuff, like the ice bucket challenge, or these other things that become huge social ways of saying 'look at how nice I am', rather than actually caring about the actual cause or it being a personal thing to you.*

DW: There are definitely people who do it for that reason.

SP: *But it's the damnation of those who don't take part that scares me. The fact that you've not done this therefore means you're horrible.*

DW: I had one of those charity muggers – I don't even know what they're actually called because everyone just calls them charity muggers... I guess, street teams? I was in a hurry, I had to get somewhere and I thought I'll just get a cab. I hailed the cab and it was slowing down, and then one of the guys just came up with a clipboard and a bright red jacket, and he just went, 'Sorry sir...' I can't remember what it was. It wasn't this, but let's say it was African orphans. And he went, 'Hi, would you mind? Have you got a minute?' And I went, 'Ah—' I was trying to be really polite, I went, 'I haven't, you know, I've got to get somewhere.' The cab had just slowed down now, and I said, 'I've really just got to get in this cab.' And the guy looked at me and went, 'Yeah? Well I'm just trying to save a life.' And I was like, whoa! By getting a cab I'm not *not* trying to save a life.

SP: *There's a great Aziz Ansari bit where he's saying he got stopped outside a Jamba Juice and someone was like, 'Can you spare a minute for gay rights?' And he says, 'I'm just going into this Jamba Juice, I can't, blah blah,' and the guy got angry. Obviously he didn't, but the story goes Ansari turned round and said, 'A guy that works in that Jamba Juice committed a gay hate crime on a friend of mine so I'm going in there to stab him, and I've got another knife – have you got a minute for gay rights?' It's just a beautiful way of saying you can't assume that just because they're not signing your clipboard they're not taking action.*

DW: I always like that Jimmy Carr joke where he goes, 'I was walking down the street and a lady came up to me and said, "Have you got two minutes for Cancer Research?" So I said, "Yes, of course, yeah, but I don't think we'll get much done."'

EDDY TEMPLE-MORRIS

Make your hate mean something

Or, life's too short

SP: *I've always loved your wonderful enthusiasm and excitement, exploding to play this new track. But what made me realize that we were truly going to connect and be friends was seeing on Twitter or Facebook ranting about your hatred of Muse, which I instantly connected with. I'd only ever heard you be so positive, because, I guess, if it's your radio show why would you be addressing anything negative? You're using that airtime to talk about the stuff you're in love with and obsessed with, so* *it was wonderfully exciting to then hear you railing against Muse, who I'm not a fan of. A lot of people are; I don't get it myself.*

ETM: Let's turn this into a positive, because that's very interesting, you talking about positivity and use of airtime. The most interesting and valuable lesson that MTV taught me was that for every person that loves you, there's someone who hates you. And the hate that I would get would be largely twofold. Either people would have a problem with me because they saw me as posh, or they would have a problem with me because they saw me as too positive. And it's a very English thing, I think, because of where England is in the world, the latitude of it and the temperament. If you look at it historically, England is quite good at depression. The further north you go the more cynical and depressed you get. The Brits love a bit of hate. And a lot of them hate positivity and I would frequently get messages from people going, 'You're so fucking positive, you just make me sick. Why are you always saying you love stuff? That's what I hate about your show, and you.' Why the hell would use however many hours I've got on my show to play a record I hate?

SP: *Or to address it in any way...*

ETM: I have a history of turning big stuff down and one of the many things I turned down was the drivetime show here (at Xfm), and I turned it down because of that: I just can't bring myself to play a Muse record twice a day or a record that doesn't connect with me or I don't feel at all and I have to say is good, or lie.

SP: *If you look at my social media now you'll rarely find me slagging things off because there are so many things I want to shout about and get excited about. The same thing – you've got a radio show. You've got this limited amount of time and space. Why wouldn't you just fill it with the stuff you're most excited and buzzing about.*

ETM: Yeah. Back in 2013 when I was really, really low, I still had to go on air. There was a period of about three weeks when I couldn't go on air and I got someone else to do my show for a bit. But there was a period where I was going on, and this guy was a listener and he somehow could just tell that I was really, really down. And he said, 'You don't sound right at the moment – is everything OK?' I ended up talking to him. And we've actually since become friends. He said to me, 'Listen man: I've had this awful thing I've been through – I found out my wife was having several affairs, we've got kids and everything's gone completely tits up and I wanted to kill myself. And the thing that stopped me from killing myself was you. And just listening to your show every week and your endless enthusiasm and positivity made me think, you know what, there is at least music to live for. And you literally saved my life, so thank you so much.'

I was so deeply moved by that that then the boundary between listener and presenter then just vaporized and we became friends. We ended up meeting, going for dinner and becoming really good mates. That's really profound and that comes down to what we're talking about.

I connected with you on the same thing. You've said frequently that you preface tweets: 'I don't like to be negative, but...' And then you say something charming, basically. If you hate all the time it doesn't mean anything. If you're very positive and you do hate now and again then it does mean something.

SP: *It has become the default to spend a lot of time hating. I've probably heard two Miley Cyrus songs and probably two Justin Bieber songs so I'm not a fan of them, but I don't have the energy to have the amount of hatred people have for them. It's just not something I'm exposed to. I don't need to waste my time. I've got a lot of friends who are heavily tattooed or tattoo artists and there was a TV show about tattoo addiction, and, being a fan of good tattoo art I didn't watch it. But I watched on Twitter as all these people watched it purely to make themselves get angry at how shit and poor a representation this programme was. Don't put yourself through that! You could have watched a good documentary in that time. You could have gone for a walk!*

ETM: Yeah, life's too short. Go for a walk and look up. I make a real point when I'm walking around to try not to look at my phone and to try to look up. I've made a real, conscious effort to do it and I started noticing all of these amazing things. When you're walking round, try not to look down at your phone all the time because you could walk past the love of your life and not even realize you're doing that.

TALL DARK FRIEND

Educating the next generation

Or, the problem-solving powers of the human brain

TDF: I just did a week in a primary and junior school teaching trans-awareness and music therapy at the same time. It was the most privileged thing I've ever done. It was so fantastic. They just get it. They just get it straight away. They've got the best questions. You answer once, and it's like 'OK, sure'. The most lewd thing I think anyone asked me was the size of my boobs and how big they were going to get. There was no giggling or snickering, they were just listening intently.

SP: *That's why it's so crucial to teach all of these things at school level: no one knows what you shouldn't maybe ask. You just ask anything. So that was part of the Educate and Celebrate scheme – is that a local thing, or a national thing?*

TDF: It's being rolled out at the moment, from my understanding. It was a flagship scheme at Malden Primary School and it went very, very well, and it was an independent company that's been taken on as a government scheme. So it's going from strength to strength. And I'm now hoping they'll stick me in secondary schools, because I'm quite ready for that barrage of confusion. I'd like to really get in there and dig through the sniggering and laughing and just get to the core of that. Because that is going to be a different thing entirely: that's going to be carnage.

SP: *Completely different. In that situation, that's the one that's going to be that bit more thankless, because the people you do reach are more* *likely to be going home and having these realizations, rather than saying it in front of their classmates or anything else. There will be loads that are talking shit and being offensive, drawing pictures of anything obscene, but what will be exciting and interesting is that it will be the ones who you reach that you possibly don't know you've reached that would be the most important.*

TDF: Yes, absolutely. There is that age, that turnover from junior to senior school. When we finished the week, we went and flew multicoloured kites in the field. It was LGBT [lesbian, gay, bisexual and transgender] week, so it was an LGBT celebration. We had to walk through their senior school to get to this field, and it was this really weird atmosphere. Everyone was staring at me. I've got a bit of an Afro as well, but I am quite obviously transgender – I'm not blessed in all areas. But these kids were staring, and the toddlers that have been with me all week, they're involved now, they're totally happy with everything, they're saying to me, 'Do you know they're looking at you?' And they're confused: their older brothers and sisters are staring. Well, it's like, that's now your responsibility. You're going to be in that school next year. It was weird to think they had this sense that they would now go home and talk to their older brothers and sisters about it. And I've heard little anecdotes from the teachers that this has gone on – that they've gone home and educated their families about it.

SP: *That is so exciting and so important as well. Again, not to shit on the area that we've both grown up in, but that's really important for educating the people that you can't reach. I used to work in HMV in Beckton and there was a security guard there who was a big, really gruff skinhead guy, and my manager who took him on there was like, 'Give him a chance.' And I remember he was the first person that came in to me and said, 'Pip, I was reading poetry last night, and I found a poem named "The Scroobius Pip". Was that where you got your name?' Of all the people to call me out on where it came from... He was formerly a card-carrying member of the BNP [British National Party] and it turned out he'd educated himself on this and was saving up to have his tattoo of a bulldog with a Union Jack erased. A few years down the line, we went round his house where he lived with his dad, and we took a black friend of ours.*

The thing that impressed me the most was he had been brought up to be racist, essentially. He'd pulled himself out of it and then he'd gradually started to turn his 60-year-old dad around, who'd spent 60 years thinking that black people were leaching off society and were trouble, and turned everyone around.

That inspires me way more than someone like myself who happens to have been brought up by liberal parents who've taught me everyone is equal. It's more impressive when I see people who it would be completely fair if they were racist idiots or bigoted idiots, because that is what they have grown up around. So what's exciting about working with the younger kids is that hopefully then it can climb up the ladder in some way.

TDF: That story of your friend, it's a testament to the problem-solving powers of the human brain. They're indoctrinated by a group of people, they didn't then move to a group of people who gave them an opposing viewpoint. The neutral state of the brain elevated them or they elevated themselves out of it. It wasn't another indoctrination.

SP: *It was actually going, 'That's illogical.'*

TDF: Surely that says something about the state of right and wrong in these situations; that the brain arrives at a place of peace and understanding – not tolerance, because that's not a word that needs to be used; it's not something that needs to be tolerated.

SP: *It does feel, in our area, like it's a case of education and that's why it's important. It hadn't even crossed my mind – this is going to sound really stupid – that these junior school kids are going to grow up. It was literally, 'Oh, you're teaching it to young kids and then you'll teach it to older kids.' But no: they will become older kids. That's the beautiful thing, that next year they will be the ones that at this point would be sniggering and laughing. So if you're going to the schools in years to come, it will leave that much more acceptance all the way along.*

TDF: Sending them out into the world. It is wonderful.

GAIL PORTER

Funny mummy

Or, the kids are alright

SP: *Your alopecia was very well publicized. Saying you embraced it sounds wrong, but you were very much not going to wear hats and wigs, which for someone whose hair was like yours...*

GP: My hair was a big feature. I've still got it, by the way. I've got it in a jar. I kept it. How it all started was, I was filming a programme called *Dead Famous* in America, where we looked for famous people who were dead, doing seances – the clue is in the title. We were in Vegas; I think we were looking for Frank Sinatra. I remember getting up, having a shower, I was washing my hair not paying much attention... And I felt the water go up to my ankles. And I thought, oh, something's blocking the plug. And it was my hair. I had a look and huge lumps had just come out. I thought, don't panic, don't panic. My daughter was actually staying with my ex-husband at the time because I was just away for three weeks. So I left with a full head of hair, then by the end of the three weeks in Vegas I was completely bald. There was a tiny bit left, which I made into a little Mohican and I dyed it pink. I was hysterical. I phoned my ex-husband and said, 'You're going to have to brace Honey, because Mummy's gone away with a full head of hair and Mummy's coming back with nothing – in three weeks.' He said, 'Oh shut up, you're joking.' And I said, 'It's not really that funny.'

SP: *Yeah, it's not a joke.*

GP: And if I'm going to make up something funny, it's not going to be, Mummy's going to come back bald. I still had my eyelashes and eyebrows at that point – they all came off as well. I went out the night I did my Mohican thing. It was the last night in Vegas and we went to this really cool club, and I was so self-conscious and just thinking I looked horrific. But all these cool kids came over and were like, 'Oh my God, you're really cool.' They thought I'd done it on purpose. So suddenly that gave me a bit of confidence. They said, 'What do you do?' And I went, 'I am in a band.' I was just loving it. I was getting cocktails in, business cards, guys saying, 'Here's my card, we should hang out, you look really cool.'

But then reality hits the next day, when you wake up and think, I've got a jar full of hair, and I'm going home to deal with my daughter. I cried all the way home on the flight.

SP: *That's a long flight as well.*

GP: Exactly. So then my ex-husband opened the door and went, 'Shit man, you're bald.' And I said, 'I told you.'

SP: *This wasn't a joke.*

GP: He was shocked. My daughter was tiny, she was, what, two? And she literally saw me and went: 'Rock 'n' roll!' I said, 'Do you like it?' She said, 'Funny Mummy!' And I just thought, you know what, it's OK.

SP: *The simplicity of that, after it being such a make or break moment for you... You'd rung to say 'can you brace her?' and had kind of been laughed at, essentially. And children are the ones who, quite rightfully, can completely innocently crush you. She could have gone, 'You look hor-rible,' not meaning it, not knowing the damage it would do.*

GP: Yeah, like you said, it's something so simple. The person that means the most to me in my entire life, if she likes it, then I don't give a fuck what anyone else thinks.

SP: *You became an ambassador for the Little Princess Trust; my girl-friend, at least once now, maybe twice, has grown her hair and cut it off and donated it because they make wigs for little princesses, essen-tially – children who've either got alopecia or who are going through cancer treatment.*

GP: They make wigs; wigs are very expensive, really expensive. The strangest thing I did once was go to this house to meet with – this was not to do with the Little Princess Trust – a little girl who had no hair. And she was five or six, and had alopecia. I went to meet her parents. And the mum and dad, they were so stressed, going, 'This is the worst thing ever.' And I said, 'Oh is she really traumatized by it?' The kid was fine: it was Mum and Dad. They said, 'Do you have a boyfriend?' And at the time I did, and they were like, 'Oh, God, we were really worried because of the way she looks, but you've managed to get one?' Managed?! I was so offended. I didn't want to say anything, but no wonder this kid... I 'managed' to get one. I said, 'Do you know what, I've still got the same heart, same soul – just because I haven't got my hair.' And that made me more determined than ever to stay as I was. I went to pick the little one up from her ballet class and she was dancing away with all her friends, and she was completely bald. She came over to me and I said, 'You'll never guess: you and me have got something exactly the same.' She went, 'Oh! Did you get a new camera for Christmas too?' She was completely oblivious.

SP: *With my stutter I found out only years and years after having it, it came from when I almost drowned as a child. I was unaware of that, because after that happened my parents played it down. My big memory of it is my dad coming out into the sea; he brought me back and I remember him saying, 'Oh you've ruined me new trainers,' and joking about it. My parents were aware that as a child I'd be over that in a second; soon as I'd got an ice cream in my hand, or a slice of pizza, that's dealt with. At least externally – there may be some internal; as I said, it turned into a stutter, but... The fact that there's a child that, again, a child can handle that kind of thing – it's the parents that have to be the ones to go, 'Right, this is fine.'*

GP: After they said I'd managed to get a boyfriend, I started blanking out the conversation because I was so shocked. They were talking among themselves saying, 'She could possibly get married.' I was thinking, she's five! Do you know what, you shouldn't be worrying about her getting married anyway – been there, done that, it's very expensive. So yeah, don't even bother. She's there, she's beautiful, she's happy.

And you're congratulating me on managing to get laid and wondering if she's going to get married. What's wrong with you people?

TOM ROBINSON

You've got to hide your love away
Or, it was always the wrong pronoun

TR: It's always hard for kids to find themselves drawn to someone of the same sex, whatever environment they grow up in. Even today. Even with all the resources we have. Growing up in a heterosexual environment with heterosexual influences it's quite hard for kids to find their own identity and mark it out for themselves. But I think in the fifties and sixties when I grew up it was that much harder because it was illegal.

SP: *I was going to say, until '67 it was illegal to be gay.*

TR: Yes, you'd get four years in prison. Bizarrely, after they legalized homosexual acts in private between two men aged twenty-one or over, there were more arrests for gay offences in the next ten years than there had been in the previous ten. Because it had been defined, the police could then find all kinds of reasons, whether you've broken the law as it's defined. Two men kissing in public was an act of gross indecency. And it was prosecutable. And people were prosecuted for it in my time in London in the seventies, for gross indecency for kissing.

SP: *So you were growing up and starting to feel you have an attraction to people of the same sex, but you were growing up somewhere that that was not only frowned upon but it's also illegal. How do you start to get through that?*

TR: For starters, there weren't any gay role models. So there had been Noël Coward, who everybody in the London set or the literary circles, they knew he was gay; they got the gay references in his plays, his comic songs. But growing up as a teenager in rural Wessex, I had no idea that that was even out there, and they couldn't be open about it because of the threat of legal action. So those of us who were due to grow up and have a happy life had no idea that that was in store for us. That that was even a possibility. That you could be gay – or that you could be attracted to somebody of the same sex and still have a perfectly happy life and be fulfilled, and that you were not alone. That was the great thing David Bowie said, in 1972, 1973, when he did that whole Ziggy 'coming out' thing. When he sang, 'You're not alone.' That resonated in a million bedsits across the country.

SP: *Completely. I need to just drive that home a little bit because it's so hard to comprehend in today's society, a time where you wouldn't have even particularly known what these feelings were, because it was so not out there and not discussed.*

TR: It was: in a negative way. You heard about 'queers'. Your parents warned you about queers. Other kids at school made jokes about queers. And if anybody, any boy showed some level of affection to another boy in a friendly way at school: 'Oh, homos!' It was – and you used to join in that to try and draw the heat off yourself – it was horrendous, the self-hate.

SP: *It's the classic thing there, the self-hate or the over-exaggeration of that because of your own wanting to cover up. Or even not wanting to accept it.*

TR: We knew what it was and we knew it was bad. So we were kind of warned about homosexuals before we even knew we were one. So that's why, in the end, I think just trying to take my life seemed the simplest way out of it.

SP: *What age were you?*

TR: I was just sixteen. I'd just turned sixteen. I had just joined the sixth form and I couldn't see any way forward. I would rather have died than anyone find out that I was in love with this other boy at school. I was just obsessively, passionately, massively in love. Never told him. He had no idea but I had this worshipping obsession from afar.

SP: *That's something again, when people don't talk to their gay friends about these taboo things. That realization that it's not necessarily a waking up and going 'I like boys', it's waking up and going 'I'm in love with THAT boy'. It's not 'this is now an exciting thing', it's 'I'm in love with this person who happens to be the same sex'.*

TR: The wrong sex.

SP: *Yeah the wrong sex for what I happen to have been brought up to believe I should be attracted to. You didn't have any gay role models when you were growing up, so you went out and became one.*

TR: Well it was what David Bowie did for me. Basically all through the sixties I was a mad passionate music fan; buying records, listening to records, learning records, singing, being in bands, all the rest of it. Then completely divorced from that was my emotional life where I was fixated upon and attached to other boys. And none of the music I heard had anything to do with the emotions I was feeling. It was always almost but not quite. So when John Lennon sang, 'Hey you've got to hide your love away'. I'd go, 'Yes, I know all about that', then he'd go, 'If she's gone I can't go on', and I'd sigh. A song called 'You've Got to Hide Your Love Away' – I'd like to make a radio show based on that as a theme. But that was the thing. It was almost what you felt, but the pronouns were wrong. So nothing was documenting our loves. And it wasn't until David Bowie came along in 1972, with 'Hunky Dory', 'Ziggy Stardust', all those songs – and said openly in *Melody Maker* 'I'm bisexual, actually' that it kind of opened this valve for a whole generation who had no expression. And we followed Bowie like crazy. We bought every record, read his every pronouncement, because he was telling our story for the first time. You'd listen to a great record – this is the key thing – not just some shit record that some gay person happened to have made. It was a brilliant, top class world-beating record, and it was about us!

SP: *And that is the key there: his sexuality was the footnote rather than the determining thing. There's a lot of stuff, particularly in the gay scene in the late seventies and eighties, where the key factor was that they were gay. Yeah there were some alright songs but the main part was 'we're gay and proud and open'. And that was the exciting thing about Bowie: he happened to be bisexual, but look at this amazing iconic music.*

TR: If his music had been shit, nobody would have given a toss what his sexuality was. You listen to a song like 'The Bewlay Brothers', this mysterious story about this bromance going on in the dark shadows of the London underground scene. Who knew what it was about – turned out to be about his own brother, Terry. But it was something we could all project on to and I swore to myself, if I could ever do that for somebody else – if I ever got into a position with my own music, which I had ambitions for, but no hope of doing at the time – if I ever got to the position with my own music where I could do for someone what Bowie had done for me, then I'd do my best.

STEWART LEE

Existing in the moment

Or, no, it's not on YouTube

SP: *On Wikipedia, entries are divided up and there's a 'known for' section. Yours had* Fist of Fun, Richard not Judy, Jerry Springer: The Opera *and* Comedy Vehicle. *And it occurred to me what you're essentially known for isn't a tangible thing that they can tag on Wikipedia. You might want to say all those are important points in your career, but for me, what you're known for is stand-up. It's shows, night after night and year after year. I found it fascinating: it's rare that there's something that they can't just tag to and link to. They can't say, 'Known, in general, for being a consistent comedian.'*

SL: It's not documented. I did do two telly shows in the mid-nineties with Rich Herring as a double act, but all through the nineties – well, from 1989 onwards – I was working as a stand-up two hundred nights a year on the London club circuit.

I suppose the thing about the nineties, it's hard to believe now, but first of all there wasn't YouTube; secondly, not everyone had a camera phone or equipment to edit their own film with themselves on a laptop. So it wasn't really documented. I did solo shows in Edinburgh in '94, '96, '98, '99 and 2000, and I did little tours of them round art centres and stuff – I haven't even got audios of them. It didn't occur to anyone to record them. No one really thought that the distribution networks would ever exist to make it worth doing that, whether free or commercial; or that the technology would be cheap enough to burn CD-Rs or stream things.

It's rather like the early days of rock 'n' roll and all that old seventies reggae that's now collector's items: it was just junk. We didn't really think anyone would be interested, so it didn't really occur to anyone to document it. So on Wikipedia where it says 'known for these' – they're the things that survived.

SP: *I think comedy is an almost unique art form in that sense. It's some-thing I noticed the first time I did the Fringe – I was blown away by a lot of shows and it was that realization that the vast majority of those shows aren't going to turn into a DVD or something that's distributed. Then next year, there will be a completely new show, so that show that I saw that was absolutely amazing only existed in that moment. And that is unique to comedy. With music, it's stuff that will be repeated and you likely play a lot of the same songs over time. Even a lot of the more unique moments of jazz – not that they would be repeated necessarily, but you would riff over the same bits again and you'd get that same feeling from it.*

SL: It's really wonderful to hear you say that about the Edinburgh Fringe because it's not just comedy, it's like 700 comedy shows and 1,400 other shows of theatre and other things, but that's what I think about it every year.

When I was a little kid my mum used to read me a book called *The Folk of the Faraway Tree* by Enid Blyton. People would climb up this tree and every week a different cloud would be at the top of it. And in that cloud there was a whole world, then that cloud would blow away and another cloud would come with an entirely different world in it. And you could never see that world again; it was gone. And that's what Edinburgh's like. You can't explain to people. So when you read a journalist doing an overview of it... Did they see a show a day? So thirty shows. Did they see two shows a day – sixty shows? Even if they saw a hundred, it's not even one per cent of what was on. So you can never get to the bottom of it. And to know that those things will pass and not come back I think is incredibly thrilling in the world we live in now, where everything is documented and cross-platform and multi-format. The idea that things will be gone just doesn't exist any more.

SP: *It makes things more valuable.*

SL: I went to see *The Snowman* at Christmas with my kids. Obviously, when the Snowman starts flying, it's really great. The Snowman flies up in the air, and then some mum who'd been yacking all the way through – it was full of horrible middle-class parents – she got a camera phone out to film the flying Snowman, and then the security guard came and said, 'You can't film,' and that was the big moment of that show. That was the moment it had built towards, where all the kids go, 'Ah, he's flown!' And it's gone, because I ended up in the middle of this dispute. Why was she doing that? Why would she want to do that, at that moment? We've got a culture where people have to see things through a little lens to realize they're really happening. We've got to get back— the primacy of the live performance isn't the same as all that stuff.

SP: *I think it's a weird thing in society – the need for acknowledgement of anything you've done; with Facebook, with checking into places just to say you went into a building. Years ago, when I was a teenager, I'd been doing photography for a while and I went on holiday with my dad and his girlfriend, and she couldn't understand that I didn't take any photos. And I said, 'Well, I love taking photos but I don't do it as proof that I've been somewhere.' I don't need a reel of proof – I'll tell my friends I've been somewhere. I don't need to prove it. They'll hopefully take me on my word, not go, 'Nah, you didn't go to Turkey.'*

SL: I went to make a documentary for Radio 4 about Native American clowning in New Mexico, about ten years ago. Normally they don't let gringos in, but there was this one weekend in Taos where the Taos Indians let you see the clown ritual. It's quite a big thing. They are over the whole village, but there's a no photography rule. As you go into the reservation, they search you for phones, cameras, recording devices. Because one hundred years ago when the first cameras were filming these events, it was decided they were obscene and they all got closed down because the evidence existed for Washington to say, 'We can't have them doing all this crazy stuff.'

What was brilliant about that was amazing stuff was happening, huge spectacles, but it was the first time in about a decade where I wasn't looking through a forest of raised hands. And I remember the whole thing really vividly. I remember the sky being really blue, and I remember the colours and smells and tastes. I think it's partly because, subconsciously, my brain was saying to me, there's no other record of this. No one is ever going to film this, it's not allowed. So you've got to remember it. I still smoked then, and, recounting it now, I can feel how hard it was to breathe as a smoker at that altitude in hot weather, for example. It's really vivid in a way that it wouldn't be if you were documenting it all.

SP: *I found it a lot this year with Glastonbury: I love Glastonbury, but this was the first year it felt more of a TV show that happened to have people there than a festival. Dan and I played on Billy Bragg's stage, which was amazing for me because I'm a big Billy Bragg fan, and I did a post about it. And I was stunned at the amount of people who said, 'Where can I listen to this?' or 'Where can I view this?' Well, you can't, because you weren't there. It just seems alien for people to think that something where they weren't there, they can't now just access it. You need to come out to it. There are so few things in the world now that exist just in the moment. And that's a beautiful thing, I think, that needs to be preserved.*

NOW IT'S YOUR TURN

SO YOU WANNA BE AN ULTIMATE PODCASTER?

Right then... As I said in the Introduction, one of the things that excites me about podcasting is that it gives a voice to anyone who wants one: you don't have to be backed by a billion-dollar corporation or have a CV full of previous hosting gigs. If you have something to say then you can have a podcast.

Now, that doesn't mean it will be a good podcast, or a popular one. But I never promised that. If you want to start a podcast for fame and fortune then you should probably look elsewhere. The reality is, most podcasts, either at the start or for their whole runs, are done for the love of it. For the chance to feed that need to get your idea out there.

So I figured it would be good to tell you about the kit I use and the platforms, and all that good stuff. Let's start with a kit list:

1 x BOSS BR-800 digital recorder

1 x Samson S-phantom power DI box

2 x sE Magneto cardioid condenser microphones

2 x weighted desk microphone stands

4 x XLR cables

1 x multi-socket extension lead

I should start by saying that ALL of this was recommended to me, with multiple options, by the one and only Mr Dan Le Sac, so any apparent technical knowledge shown in the next few paragraphs is all sucked through his wisdom straw.

Right, let's start with the all-important BOSS BR-800. This is basically a little self-contained mixing desk. You can put a massive memory card in it and then record all your stuff directly on there. This was key to me as I'm hugely paranoid of laptops crashing during long recording sessions and, since I don't take a tech or anyone with me, I didn't want to have to worry about that. The key thing for me with this unit was that it will record multiple separate streams. So, if the guest wasn't as close to the mic as me, or whatever, it can be played with when Worgie or Buddy Peace are mastering it. While I have headphones on during each interview, I'm not spending THAT much time monitoring or live mixing as my focus is on the guest, so the more that can be tweaked in post-production, the better.

Next up are the sE Magneto cardioid condenser microphones, which use phantom power, hence the Samson S-phantom, which powers them both. These are right little beauties. I really like how warm they sound and how well they pick everything up. The reason I also carry the weighted desk mic stands is so I can just point these at the guest and let them do their work. Remember, when guests hold the mic themselves (which is sometimes unavoidable) over a 60 to 90 minute conversation, they may not always keep it facing them or the same distance or whatever. So I find, when I can, if I can just get it on a stand and pointing at them (between me and them) then, as long as they are talking in my direction, we are all good.

The XLR cables are just to wire the mics and the BR-800 together and all that (but Worgie would say I need to spend more on mine as I often have crackles).

The final bit of kit I felt worth listing is simply a multi-plug extension lead. Because, well, they're cheap and small and really damn handy. You WILL need power and if you are recording in different locations it's risky to assume there will always be power exactly where you need it. So it's way better to be that little bit over-prepared to make it easy on everyone.

I've left off headphones as I've gone through numerous pairs – losing them, breaking them – and now I just carry a mini jack-to-jack adaptor so I can just plug in whatever headphones I have on me (I ALWAYS have headphones on me as I listen to hours and hours of podcasts that AREN'T my own each week).

Now I've listed it all I need to make one thing clear:

YOU DON'T NEED ANY OF THIS.

This is what I use, and I'm real happy with it, but podcasts are recorded in so many different ways and with way smaller set-ups:

A ZOOM mobile recording unit with a couple of mics plugged in sounds great.

A ZOOM without mics plugged in sounds pretty damn decent, too.

Hell, I've heard podcasts that have literally MILLIONS of listeners get recorded on iPhones. That's the beauty of this medium: it bends to your needs or budget.

Once recorded you should be mixing and making it sound as nice as you can on whatever program you can get your hands on. Worgie (and now Buddy Peace, who has taken those reins) tends to use Logic. But you CAN do it on GarageBand or a million other simple little programs.

The final step is getting it out there.

A lot of people use SoundCloud and stuff like that, which is great but I for some reason find that a little restrictive. When I moved *Distraction Pieces* over to Acast it felt like the perfect home. Acast is a podcast app that hosts and distributes podcasts. They also bring in sponsors, which are super helpful with that whole staying constant/delivering every week thing.

The cool thing about Acast is when uploading you can insert images and links and all sorts of other stuff into specific points of the conversation. So if people are listening on Acast they can then find out more or see relevant images to whatever you're talking about. It's not essential, though, if you're not into it.

The other handy thing about Acast is it puts your podcast all over the place. So, after I upload to Acast, it goes up everywhere, including the all-important iTunes.

Now, love or hate Apple, iTunes is where the vast majority of the WORLD are listening to their podcasts. So, for me, not being on iTunes would be ridiculous for the spreading of what I'm putting out.

But, I'll say it again:

YOU DON'T HAVE TO DO ANY OF THIS!

This is a medium that is growing and growing as I type this, and more and more options are appearing every day. So, however you choose to do it, make sure you ACTUALLY do it.

It's really that simple.

CONTRIBUTORS

Riz Ahmed – 25, 146

Riz Ahmed is an English actor and rapper who has starred in films including *The Reluctant Fundamentalist, The Road to Guantánamo, Four Lions, Nightcrawler* and the upcoming *Star Wars: Rouge One*. He co-founded the Hit & Run night, which is one of Manchester's leading underground music events.

Akala – 80, 149, 154, 164

Akala (real name Kingslee James Daley) is an English rapper and poet. He was presented with a MOBO award in 2006 for Best Hip-Hop Act. Besides his musical career, Akala is a vocal activist against racism and champion of equality.

Blindboy – 127, 195

Blindboy Boatclub, is one half of music and comedy award-winning Irish band The Rubberbandits (Twitter handle: @Rubberbandits). The band conceal their identities with plastic bags and are primarily a stage and television satirical act, referring to their movement as 'Gas Cuntism'.

Billy Bragg – 50, 71, 73, 161

Billy Bragg is an English singer-songwriter and activist. He is a vocal opponent of racism, sexism, bigotry and homophobia. His music is heavily centred on bringing about change and getting young people involved in activist causes.

Russell Brand – 172

Russell Brand is an English comedian, actor, radio host, author and activist. He is well known for his political activism and speaks regularly on topics including wealth inequality, corporate capitalism and media bias. He is the author of several books and has appeared in numerous films, most notably *Despicable Me* and *Get Him to the Greek*.

Adam Buxton – 3, 4, 67, 69

Adam Buxton is an English comedian, writer, actor and podcaster. He formed one half of the duo *Adam and Joe* with Joe Cornish, and the pair presented regularly on BBC Radio 6 Music. Adam hosts *Bug*, a live show that explores intriguing and noteworthy music videos through YouTube comments..

Nick Frost – 59

Nick Frost is a British actor, comedian, screenwriter, producer and author. He is best known for his work in the Three Flavours Cornetto trilogy of films with Simon Pegg: *Shaun of the Dead, Hot Fuzz* and *The World's End.*

Dr Suzi Gage – 117, 177

Researcher Dr Suzi Gage investigates the associations between substance use and mental health at the University of Bristol. She is an active blogger for the *Guardian* and her own blog, *Sifting the Evidence*, won the Good Thinking Society's first UK Science Blog Prize in 2012. Suzi has her own podcast called *Say Why to Drugs.*

Richard Herring – 11, 101

Richard Herring is an award-winning English comedian celebrated for his stand-up shows *Talking Cock, Hitler Moustache* and *Happy Now?* He is recognized as a pioneer of comedy podcasting and was one half of the nineties double act Lee and Herring (with Stewart Lee).

Rufus Hound – 19, 57, 103, 169

Rufus Hound is an English comedian, actor and presenter. He plays a ficitonalized version of himself in the CBBC TV series *Hounded*, and since 2012 has presented a BBC Radio 4 programme called *My Teenage Diary* in which celebrities talk about their teenage diaries.

Robin Ince – 35

Robin Ince is an English comedian, actor and writer. He is best known for *The Infinite Monkey Cage* on BBC Radio 4, which he co-presents with Brian Cox. In 2011, the show won a Gold Award in the Best Speech Programme category of the Sony Radio Awards.

Stewart Lee – 21, 210

Stewart Lee is an English stand-up comedian, writer, director and musician who made his name in the mid-nineties as one half of the radio duo Lee and Herring (with Richard Herring). Lee has a reputation for being 'politically correct' and often explores the trope of 'political correctness gone mad' for comic effect.

Josie Long – 6

British comedian Josie Long began performing stand-up aged 14. She won the BBC New Comedy Award aged 17 and has been nominated for the Edinburgh Comedy Award for Best Show three times. She has produced two short comedy films with director Doug King, which were nominated for a BAFTA Scotland New Talent Award.

Zane Lowe– 86, 110

Zane Lowe is a New Zealand-born award-winning radio DJ, record producer and television presenter. He rose to prominence through presenting on Xfm and MTV Europe, before hosting a new global music show on BBC Radio 1. Lowe now hosts his own show on Apple's international radio station, Beats 1.

Howard Marks – 180

Howard Marks was a Welsh drug-smuggler-turned-author who achieved notoriety through a series of high-profile court cases. He served seven years of a twenty-five year prison sentence and became known as 'Mr Nice' after he purchased a passport from convicted murderer Donald Nice. He campaigned publicly for changes in drugs legislation – namely to legalize cannabis. He died in 2016.

Killer Mike – 135, 139

Michael Render, better known by his stage name Killer Mike, is an American hip-hop recording artist and activist, and one half of the hip-hop duo Run the Jewels. He addresses themes of racism and police brutality in his music, and has written and spoken about social justice on numerous occasions.

Alan Moore – 41, 44, 187

Alan Moore is an English writer primarily known for his graphic novels and comic books including *Watchmen, V for Vendetta* and *From Hell*. He is also an occultist and ceremonial magician, and is known for being an anarchist.

Amanda Palmer – 39, 75, 76, 91

Amanda Palmer is an American singer-songwriter who first rose to fame as part of the duo The Dresden Dolls. She is the lead singer of Amanda Palmer and the Grand Theft Orchestra and is known for her controversial lyrics and performances. She has won several awards, including the Boston Music Awards Artist of the Year in 2010.

Sara Pascoe – 9, 17

Sara Pascoe is an English writer, stand-up comedian and actress. Her first book, *Animal: The Autobiography of a Female Body*, was published in 2016. She appears regularly on television shows and panels including *Mock the Week*, and *Have I Got News For You*. Pascoe is a feminist and a patron of the British Humanist Association.

Simon Pegg – 30, 107

Simon Pegg is an English actor, comedian, screenwriter and producer best known for co-writing and starring in the Three Flavours Cornetto trilogy of films: *Shaun of the Dead*, *Hot Fuzz* and *The World's End*. He has also appeared in massive movie franchises, including *Star Wars*, *Star Trek* and *Mission Impossible*. He has won numerous acting awards for his work.

Gail Porter – 121, 204

Gail Porter is a Scottish television presenter and a former model and actress. She has been open about her struggles with bipolar disorder and alopecia, and is an ambassador for the Little Princess Trust, a charity which provides wigs to children with hair loss.

Romesh Ranganathan – iv, 13, 15, 78, 79

Romesh Ranganathan is a stand-up comedian and actor. In 2013 he was nominated for Best Newcomer at the Edinburgh Comedy Awards. He presented the *Asian Provocateur* series for BBC Three in 2015, which showed him travelling to Sri Lanka to explore his ancestral roots.

Tom Robinson – 129, 207

Tom Robinson is a British singer-songwriter, bassist and radio presenter, best known for the hit songs 'Glad to be Gay' and '2-4-6-8 Motorway' with his band, also named Tom Robinson. He won a Sony Academy Award for his radio documentary *You've Got to Hide Your Love Away*, which focused on gay music.

Jon Ronson – 92, 120, 182

Jon Ronson is a Welsh journalist, documentary film-maker and radio presenter well known for his informal but sceptical research into controversial fringe politics and science. His nine books include *The Men Who Stare at Goats* and *So You've Been Publicly Shamed*, a book about the effect of the Internet age on acts of public humiliation.

Michael Smiley – 31, 33

Michael Smiley is a Northern Irish comic and actor who became well known for his role as cycle courier Tyres O'Flaherty in the cult classic TV show *Spaced*. He won Best Supporting Actor at the British Independent Film Awards and Best Actor at the Total Film Frightfest for his role in the film *Kill List*.

Kurt Sutter – 46

Kurt Sutter is an American screenwriter, producer, director and actor best known for creating the series *Sons of Anarchy*, which he wrote, produced, directed and starred in after beginning his career on crime drama *The Shield*. He wrote and appeared in *The Bastard Executioner*, which was released in 2015 and starred Scroobius Pip. In 2016, he developed a comic book mini-series entitled *Lucas Stand* and is working on a prequel to *Sons of Anarchy*.

Tall Dark Friend – 51, 201

Tall Dark Friend is the pseudonym for the transgender recording artist and author Jordan Gray. She is a pop-rock singer and is known for speaking out about her transgender life since she came out onstage at the Essex Entertainment Awards in 2014. In 2015, she rose to fame on BBC's *The Voice*.

Kate Tempest – 54

Kate Tempest is an English poet, spoken word artist and playwright. In 2013 she won a Ted Hughes Award for her epic narrative poem *Brand New Ancients*. *Everybody Down*, her debut solo album, came out in 2014 to critical acclaim and earned her a Mercury Award nomination. Her first novel, *The Bricks that Built the Houses* was published in 2016.

Eddy Temple-Morris – 124, 198

Eddy Temple-Morris is a British DJ, record producer and TV presenter. He hosted London radio station Xfm's specialist show *The Remix* for 15 years. Temple-Morris writes a weekly column for the music industry website *CMY*. He regularly DJs around Europe and has supported The Prodigy, Pendulum and Delays on their UK tours.

Frank Turner – 82, 84, 99

Frank Turner is an English singer-songwriter who was the vocalist of the post-hardcore band Million Dead before becoming an acoustic-based solo artist following the band's split in 2005. He is the author of *The Road Beneath My Feet*, named after lyrics from his song 'The Road'.

Carla Valentine – 191

Carla Valentine is a qualified anatomical pathology technologist who runs 'Dead Meet', a dating and networking group for 'death professionals'. She has her own blog and YouTube channel where she discusses her job and how she restores anatomical specimens, and she teaches students at the Academy of Forensic Medical Sciences.

Danny Wallace – 47, 197

Danny Wallace is a British film-maker, comedian, writer, actor and presenter. His notable works include the books *Join Me, Yes Man* (subsequently made into a film), *Awkward Situations for Men* and *Charlotte Street*. Wallace is a patron of the charity Build Africa.

Saul Williams – 96, 156

American actor, writer, poet and singer-songwriter Saul Williams is best known for his alternative hip-hop music, as well as his anti-war anthem 'Not in Our Name'. He has released four collections of poetry and starred in *Holler If Ya Hear Me*, a Broadway musical featuring music by murdered rapper Tupac Shakur.

INDEX

ACKNOWLEDGEMENTS

Fernando Pessoa said, 'I bear the wounds of the battles I avoided,' and I always feel acknowledgement sections end up being more about those you forget than those you remember. If your name does appear you breeze over it with a brief smile and get on with your day. If it does not and you have any reason to think it should, well, that will stick with you for days – weeks even. So for those I have forgotten please know that it was one hundred per cent intentional; take this as a declaration of war.

First and foremost I need to give mention to my agent, Becky, for pairing me up with Hannah and everyone at Octopus who have truly made this project what it is. Make no mistake; the initial seed of the idea to build this collection of thoughts came from Hannah and her team so they are more deserved of any praise for this than myself.

Then there are all the people to thank for helping keep the podcast going over the years.

Dan, Chris, Mike, Neil, Steph and everyone at Radio X for their support in my decision to go it alone.

Warren for helping me get it all off the ground and Buddy for taking the reigns of this often wild and erratic horse.

Everyone at Acast for their support and for providing an easy and accessible platform along with Jarrod and the team at BSI who help get it all up on my website in a presentable manner.

Amy and Lola for the delightful outro music (and Juno because it would be rude to leave her off).

My mum, dad, brother, Francesca and everyone else at the time that helped support what seemed like a ridiculous choice to go from an award-winning, paid show on commercial radio to a free podcast with no established audience.

Dan Le Sac for advising me on the technical side of things when I was absolutely clueless.

Joe Rogan for casually suggesting I start a podcast and still probably having no idea how big a change that caused.

Every single listener that took us from that first upload, wondering if anyone would listen, to breaking the five million downloads mark in little over a year. You made Team 3W a thing and you spread the word better than any marketing team could ever hope to do so.

Every journalist that has got onboard (Miranda Sawyer and Ben Cannon instantly come to mind but the list is way longer) and supported the podcast, widening the audience, despite us never having a press team or anyone pitching it to them.

But, most importantly, every single guest that has come on and given their time and stories. Those that are featured here, and those that are not. The openness of others is what has allowed the podcast to grow into what it has become and I am forever astounded by what each guest gives.

Finally, I dedicate everything I release to my dear friend Jamie Knott, but I would also like to dedicate this book to Mr Howard Marks, who passed as we were putting it all together. To get to share some time with him towards the end of his life, having read his stories earlier on in mine was a true honour.

Once again, if I have forgotten you here then it's definitely on purpose and means I hate you but have never had the heart to tell you.

DPP EPISODE #2
ZANE LOWE

DPP EPISODE #3

DPP #11

DPP EPISODE #1
KILLER MIKE

DPP EPISODE #14
JOSIE LONG

DP EPISODE #57
K FRIEND

DPP EP
RICHA

EPISODE #69
RT C.

DPP EPISODE #55
MORTICIAN
CARLA VALENTINE

DPP EPI
AMAND

DPP EPISODE #15